WILLIAM E. PAUL

How the Bible Became a Book

To the kind and helpful staff of my greatest writing resource—
The Wheaton Public Library

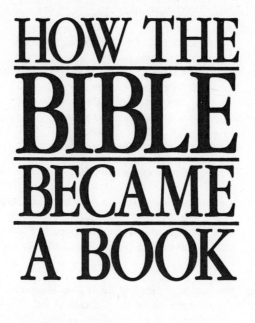

HOW THE BIBLE BECAME A BOOK

TERRY HALL

While this book is intended for the reader's personal enjoyment and profit, it is also intended for group study. A leader's guide with Reproducible Response Sheets is available from your local bookstore or from the publisher.

VICTOR BOOKS®

A DIVISION OF SCRIPTURE PRESS PUBLICATIONS INC.
USA CANADA ENGLAND

Other Books by Terry Hall

BIBLE PANORAMA
DYNAMIC BIBLE TEACHING WITH OVERHEAD TRANSPARENCIES (COOK)
FINALLY, FAMILY DEVOTIONS THAT WORK (MOODY)
GETTING MORE FROM YOUR BIBLE
HOW TO BE THE BEST SUNDAY SCHOOL TEACHER YOU CAN BE (MOODY)
MOODY BIBLE QUIZZES (VOLUMES 1–4) (MOODY)
NEW TESTAMENT EXPRESS
OFF THE SHELF AND INTO YOURSELF
OLD TESTAMENT EXPRESS
SEVEN WAYS TO GET MORE FROM YOUR BIBLE (MOODY)

Seminars by Terry Hall

Popular day-long seminars are available on Bible panorama, creative teaching, and how to get more from the Bible. Audience involvement, colorful visuals, and creative learning methods are incorporated. For more information contact: **Media Ministries,** 516 East Wakeman, Wheaton, IL 60187. (708) 665-4594

Scripture quotations are from the *Holy Bible, New International Version,* © 1973, 1978, 1984, International Bible Society. Used by Permission of Zondervan Bible Publishers.

Portions of chapter 11 drawn from "Bible Translation since John Wycliffe," by George Cowan. Christian History Magazine, vol. 2, no. 2 [nd], pp. 27ff.

Library of Congress Cataloging-in-Publication Data

Hall, Terry, 1941–
    How the Bible became a book / by Terry Hall.
        p.   cm.
    ISBN 0-89693-589-2
    1. Bible—Canon—Popular works. 2. Bible—Canon, Catholic vs. Protestant—Popular works. 3. Bible—Versions—Popular works. 4. Bible—Evidences, authority, etc.—Popular works.   I. Title.
    BS465.H33   1990
    220.1—dc20   88-60210
                                                                  CIP

1 2 3 4 5 6 7 8 9 10 Printing/Year 94 93 92 91 90

Contents

CHARTS

1

What's So Special about the Bible?

The Bible's Uniqueness among the World's Books

It had to be the strangest publishing project of all time.

Consider the initial production statistics: No editor or publishing house was responsible to oversee the 50 independent authors, representing 20 occupations, living in 10 countries during a 1,600-year span, working in three languages with a cast of 2,930 characters in 1,189 chapters, 31,173 verses, 774,746 words, and 3,567,180 letters. This massive volume covers every conceivable subject expressed in all literary forms, including prose, poetry, romance, mystery, biography, science, and history.

What was the final product? *Reader's Digest?* The Bible!

One evidence that the Bible is a supernatural book is the amazing unity it displays despite such wide differences among authors, cultures, and forms of expression.

The Bible is all one story. The last part of the last book in the Bible reads like the close of the story begun in the first part of the first book of the Bible. The beginnings of Genesis have their ultimate fulfillment in the Book of Revelation.

In Genesis 1, for example, God creates the heavens and

the earth, but in Revelation 21 He creates the new heavens and earth. Darkness, seas, sun, moon, pain, death, and the curse on nature in Genesis 1–3 are all replaced by better things in Revelation 20–22. Sin enters the world in Genesis 3 and is removed in Revelation 20, with all of its effects subsequently reversed. The initial triumph of the serpent is nullified by the ultimate triumph of the Saviour. Further contrasts and comparisons may be noted in Chart 2 on page 17.

From cover to cover, the Bible presents a consistent picture of the one true God, one cause of mankind's troubles (sin), and one universal remedy (the Saviour, God's Son). The Old Testament prepares the world for the Saviour promised immediately after the first human sin (Gen. 3:15).* The New Testament presents the Saviour's first coming to the world, His perfect life and sacrifice for sin, and the changes He can make in individuals who will receive Him. His second coming to establish a perfect world is promised and certain (Rev. 22:20).

Only God could have given such a book, so marked by consistency and lacking any unsolvable contradiction.

Books and the Book

Books abound. The Library of Congress has over 80 million items in its collection, including more than 22 million books. The current edition of *Books in Print* catalogs 781,292 English book titles available from 25,900 publishers. About 30,000 new titles are released yearly.

But among them all, the Bible still stands as the all-time best-seller.

Normally a book is considered a best-seller if it sells over a million copies and is translated into several other languages. The United Bible Societies estimates that nearly four

---

*All abbreviations used in this book are explained in Appendix A (pages 146–147).

billion Bibles have been published since 1815. Worldwide an annual average of 100 million Bibles are distributed, many at no cost. In the United States, Bible sales amount to $110 million annually.

Complete Bibles or parts of it have now been translated into over 1,700 languages, spoken by 90 percent of the world's population. Thousands of translators and support personnel are currently working at an ambitious goal of getting the Bible into the world's remaining 3,267 languages.

Whether comparing all-time or annual sales, there are no close seconds to the Bible. The distant seconds are classics which are related to or derived from the Bible. None of the other books of the world religions are even in the running.

Such statistics are all the more amazing in light of the many attempts to destroy the Bible in the past 3,500 years since the first Scripture was written. In A.D. 303, for example, Roman Emperor Diocletian commanded all Bibles be burned. Countless thousands of Christian believers were imprisoned, burned at the stake, or tortured to death rather than recant their faith in the living and written Word of God. Only 25 years later, Emperor Constantine, Diocletian's successor, ordered Bible scribe Eusebius to make 50 copies of the Bible at government expense! Constantine legalized Christianity in A.D. 313.

Long after its attackers have perished, the Bible's presence and power amplify the accuracy of Jesus' words, "Heaven and earth will pass away, but My words will never pass away" (Mark 13:31).

The Bible holds other world records too, such as having the most handwritten copies survive from ancient times. It was the first book printed on Gutenberg's newly invented press in 1456. The Bible is the first religious book to be taken into outer space (on microfilm by the astronauts). In 1933 the English government paid Russia $510,000 for an ancient Greek copy of the Bible, the highest price paid for any book at that time. The world's longest telegram contained the text of the New Testament sent on May 22, 1881 from New York to Chicago, where it was printed in its entirety in the *Chicago Tribune* and *Chicago Sun Times.*

Special Claims

The Bible claims to have originated from the God of the universe (2 Tim. 3:16; 2 Peter 1:20-21). Over 4,000 times Scripture itself claims to be a record of what God says. Furthermore, it boldly claims to be error-free (John 17:17).

The Koran, the only other book claiming to have divine authority, was supposedly dictated by the angel Gabriel from an eternal book in heaven to the Prophet Muhammad (Surah 2:7, 87, etc.). But the Koran contradicts itself by saying that Muhammad could neither read nor write (Surah 7:158). And the Koran lacks other evidences of being divine which the Bible possesses.

The remainder of the world's religions' sacred books are philosophical treatises which don't claim to be God-breathed, as the Bible does.

It's one thing to claim God authored the Bible and another to prove it. Not only does Scripture have internal consistency, but external evidences of its accuracy abound from the realms of science, history, archaeology, and literature.

Ahead of Its Time

Six hundred years before Christ, the Bible stated that the stars could not be numbered (Jer. 33:22). A few hundred years later Greek astronomer Hipparchus counted them and declared there were 1,056 stars. After a few hundred more years, Ptolemy verified his predecessor's count. Only after Galileo invented his telescope in 1610 was the centuries-old star count challenged. Now astronomers estimate there are over 100 *billion* stars in our galaxy and countless more beyond.

The Bible declared in the first century that each star is different (1 Cor. 15:41), a fact only recently verified by modern astralphotography. Of the millions of stars photographed to date, no two have been found to be alike.

When the ancients thought the earth was flat and supported by pillars, the Bible declared the earth was a circle hung in space upon nothing (Isa. 40:22; Job 26:7). The old theory began to crumble in the relatively recent voyages of Columbus and Magellan. But one photograph taken from the moon shows it all.

Dozens of similar scientific phenomena could be cited to show the accuracy of biblical statements which went contrary to popular belief at the time they were written. The Bible is still ahead of its time, for it describes how the world will end (2 Peter 3; Rev. 6–19).

Transforming Benefits

The Bible's power to transform lives stands as a strong witness to its divine origin. Countless millions have been converted over the centuries, many dramatically and radically, such as the murderous Saul of Tarsus being changed into Paul the Apostle. Society's greatest reforms and humanitarian efforts have come in response to spiritual renewals or the application of biblical principles to life.

"It is impossible to enslave mentally or socially a Bible-reading people. The principles of the Bible are the groundwork of human freedom" (Horace Greeley, nineteenth-century American journalist and politician). "The Bible has been the Magna Charta of the poor and oppressed. The human race is not in a position to dispense with it" (Thomas Huxley, nineteenth-century English biologist).

Let the Bible itself describe some of the benefits offered those who will read and heed it.

"But his delight is in the law of the Lord, and on His law he meditates day and night. He is like a tree planted by streams of water, which yields its fruit in season and whose leaf does not wither. Whatever he does prospers" (Ps. 1:2-3). "I have hidden your word in my heart that I might not sin against you" (Ps. 119:11).

"Your commands make me wiser than my enemies, for they are ever with me" (Ps. 119:98).

"Your statutes are my heritage forever; they are the joy of my heart" (Ps. 119:111).

"When your words came, I ate them; they were my joy and my heart's delight, for I bear your name, O Lord God Almighty" (Jer. 15:16).

"Whoever has my commands and obeys them, he is the one who loves me. He who loves me will be loved by my Father, and I too will love him and show myself to him" (John 14:21).

"But as for you, continue in what you have learned and have become convinced of, because you know those from whom you learned it, and how from infancy you have known the holy Scriptures, which are able to make you wise for salvation through faith in Christ Jesus" (2 Tim. 3:14-15).

"Therefore, get rid of all moral filth and the evil that is so prevalent and humbly accept the word planted in you, which can save you" (James 1:21).

"But the man who looks intently into the perfect law that gives freedom, and continues to do this, not forgetting what he has heard, but doing it—he will be blessed in what he does. . . . Religion that God our Father accepts as pure and faultless is this: to look after orphans and widows in their distress and to keep oneself from being polluted by the world" (James 1:25, 27).

"Consequently, faith comes from hearing the message, and the message is heard through the word of Christ" (Rom. 10:17).

"In addition to all this, take up the shield of faith, with which you can extinguish all the flaming arrows of the evil one. Take the helmet of salvation and the sword of the Spirit, which is the word of God" (Eph. 6:16-17).

"Your word is a lamp to my feet and a light for my path" (Ps. 119:105).

"For you have been born again, not of perishable seed, but of imperishable, through the living and enduring word of God. For, 'All men are like grass, and all their glory is like the flowers of the field; the grass withers and the flowers fall, but the word of the Lord stands forever.' And this is the word that was preached to you. Therefore, rid yourselves of all malice and all deceit, hypocrisy, envy, and slander of every kind" (1 Peter 1:23-25; 2:1).

If the Bible didn't exist, how much could be known about:

☐ God?

☐ Heaven or Hell?
☐ How to get safely to Heaven and escape Hell?
☐ Angels and demons?
☐ Creation?
☐ How God relates to us?
☐ Life after death?

What Others Think

Here is what some others whose lives have been changed by the Bible have said about it.

"The Scriptures are the true words of the Holy Spirit" (Clement of Alexandria, 2nd-century church theologian).

"The Scriptures are the writings of God" (Tertullian, 2nd-century church father).

"I have learned to pay [the books of Scripture] such honor and respect as to believe most firmly that not one of their authors has erred in writing anything at all" (Augustine, 4th-century church bishop).

"Never will the writings of mortal men in any respect equal the sentences inspired by God. We must yield the place of honor to the prophets and the apostles, keeping ourselves prostrate at their feet as we listen to their teachings. I would not have those who read my books, in these stormy times, devote one moment to them which they would otherwise have consecrated to the Bible" (Martin Luther, 16th-century Reformation leader).

"I am profitably engaged in reading the Bible. Take all of this Book that you can by reason and the balance by faith, and you will live and die a better man. I believe the Bible is the best gift God has ever given to man. All the good from the Saviour of the world is communicated to us through this book; but for this book we could not know right from wrong. All things desirable to man are contained in the Bible" (Abraham Lincoln, 19th-century American president).

"The Bible is the truest utterance that ever came by alphabetic letters. . . . It is the finest bit of literature ever written by the pen of men" (Thomas Carlyle, 19th-century Scottish historian).

"I have spent seventy years of my life studying that Book to satisfy my heart; it is the Word of God. The Bible is stamped with a Speciality of Origin, and an immeasurable distance separates it from all competitors. I bank my life on the statement that I believe this Book to be that solid rock of Holy Scriptures" (William E. Gladstone, 19th-century British prime minister).

"The Bible is worth all other books which have ever been printed" (Patrick Henry, 18th-century American statesman).

"The Bible is no mere book, but a living Creature, with a power that conquers all that oppose it" (Napoleon Bonaparte, 19th-century French emperor).

"There are more sure marks of authenticity in the Bible than in any profane history" (Sir Isaac Newton, 18th-century English physicist).

"I believe a knowledge of the Bible without a college course is more valuable than a college course without the Bible. The Bible has been a greater influence on the course of English literature than all the other forces put together" (William Lyon Phelps, 19th-century university president).

"It is impossible to rightly govern the world without God and the Bible" (George Washington, 18th-century American president).

"I have carefully examined the evidences of the Christian religion, and if I were sitting as a juror upon its authenticity I would unhesitatingly give my verdict in its favor" (Alexander Hamilton, 18th-century American statesman).

What would *you* write if your quotation about the value of the Bible were to be included in the next edition?

What's in Store?
If faith is only as strong as its object, how solid is the Bible as a foundation for belief about spiritual matters? How much do you know about spiritual matters? How much do you know about the original formation of the Bible?

This book has been written to help you answer some key questions about the Bible. Some of those questions are listed below, along with the numbers of chapters addressing them:

● Why does the Roman Catholic Church have more books in its version of the Bible than the Protestant Bible? Who's right, and what's in those extra books? (See chapter 6.)

● How do we know that we have the *right* books in the Bible? What about the "lost books" some popular magazines have touted? (See chapters 6 and 9.)

● What about the great books of other world religions? Every one can't be right because they contradict one another. Are the Koran or the Vedas to be followed instead of the Bible? (See chapters 1 and 12.)

● With so many versions of the Bible in English, which should be used for reading and study? Are some translations more reliable than others? Why do some Bibles delete passages or relegate them to the margin? (See chapters 9 and 10.)

● Who were the people God used to make the Bible? Did they collaborate with one another to make their works agree? (See chapters 2–5 and 7–8.)

● How would you answer an agnostic who claims there are 200,000 errors in the manuscripts of the Greek New Testament, and hence it can't be trusted? How well have the biblical records been preserved and copied? (See chapter 12.) Has the Bible text gotten garbled over the centuries? If only imperfect copies of the originals exist, what's the sense of talking about an "inspired" Bible anyway? (See chapters 10 and 12.)

To begin dealing with these and other questions, let's explore how the Bible became a book in a natural progression. See Chart 1, "The Chain of Revelation."

THE CHAIN OF REVELATION
(Chart 1)

GOD
|
|
REVELATION (God making Himself known by any means)
|
|
INSPIRATION (Scriptural writings vested with God's authority)
|
|
RECOGNITION (Scripture accepted by recipients as divine)
|
|
CANONIZATION (Bible books gradually collected into one volume)
|
|
PRESERVATION (Scripture faithfully copied for distribution)
|
|
TRANSLATION (Bible put into other languages)
|
|
OBSERVATION (People read and study the Bible)
|
|
ILLUMINATION (Holy Spirit helps people understand the Bible)
|
|
INTERPRETATION (People study what the Bible means)
|
|
APPLICATION (People use the Bible for their faith and practice)

THE BIBLE'S BEGINNING AND ENDING
(Chart 2)

GENESIS 1–4	REVELATION 19–22
God created the heavens and earth (1:1)	God creates new heavens and earth (21:1)
Light created (1:3)	Lamb is the light (21:23)
Darkness and night created (1:5)	No darkness or night (22:5)
Waters gathered into seas (1:10)	No more seas (21:1)
God made the sun and the moon (1:16)	No need of the sun or the moon (21:23)
Creation pronounced done (2:1)	New creation pronounced done (21:6)
Man's primeval home by a river (2:10)	Man's eternal home by a river (22:1)
Death for eating from a tree (2:17)	Life for eating from a tree (22:2)
Marriage of Adam (2:18-23)	Marriage of the Lamb (19:6-9)
Eve, the wife of Adam (2:22-25)	New Jerusalem, wife of Christ (21:9-10)
Serpent deceived (3:1, 13)	Serpent banned from deceiving (20:3)
Satan's first attack on man (3:1ff)	Satan's final attack (20:7-10)
Satan appeared in garden (3:1)	Satan disappears in lake of fire (20:10)
A garden which became defiled (3:6-7)	A city that can't be defiled (21:27)
Fellowship with God broken (3:8-10)	Face-to-face fellowship with God (21:3)
Initial triumph of the serpent (3:13)	Ultimate triumph of the Lamb (20:10)
Saviour's first coming promised (3:15)	Saviour's second coming promised (22:20)

GENESIS 1–4	REVELATION 19–22
Pain greatly multiplied (3:16)	No more mourning, crying, or pain (21:4)
Curse on man and nature (3:14-19)	No more curse (22:3)
Serpent's doom promised (3:15)	Serpent's doom accomplished (20:10)
Curse imposed on nature (3:17)	Curse removed from nature (22:3)
Man's dominion over nature lost (3:19)	Man's dominion restored (22:5)
First death (3:21, 4:8)	No more death, neither sorrow (21:4)
First sacrificial lamb (3:21)	Last sacrificial Lamb (21:4, 14)
First paradise closed (3:23)	New paradise opened (21:25)
Angel kept people from garden (3:24)	Angel welcomes people to city (21:9-10)
Man driven from God's presence (3:24)	Believers shall see His face (22:4)
Tree of life taken from man (3:24)	Tree of life open to man (22:14)
God's mark on Cain (4:15)	God's name on people's foreheads (22:4)
First city built by Cain (4:17)	Holy city comes from God (21:2)

2

From the Meekest to the Mightiest

The Old Testament Writers, Part 1

What do princes, priests, gatekeepers, judges, shepherds, prophets, musicians, poets, fishermen, kings, botanists, farmers, teachers, lobbyists, and other government officials have in common? God used them all to write the Scriptures.

Who are the people God used to record His written revelation for time and eternity? When and where did they live? What is known about them? How many of the 50 known Scripture writers can you name?

God set the stage for Scripture by creating people with their ability to form languages and alphabets, knowing He would communicate through them. In the beginning, God communicated directly with individuals, but in Moses' time He began to add a written record of His revelation.

Over the ages God has made Himself known by many means, including angels, His Creation, dreams, visions, and audible voice. Thoughts become more precise as they are fixed in words. The Creation conveys a general message of a powerful, intelligent Creator, but His written revelation gives the specifics about Him.

If God hadn't recorded His revelation, we would only have testimony transmitted orally over thousands of years. Realizing how garbled a message can become as it is whispered through several people, imagine the twists it could take over 20 centuries! And unless the originator of the message wrote it down, how could others verify the accuracy of what they'd received?

Written materials are also easier to duplicate with precision and to translate into other languages. Remember, the Bible began long before the invention of phonograph records, audio or video tapes, or compact discs!

The Apostle Paul describes the process of people writing Scripture as God's *inspiration* ("to breathe in", 2 Tim. 3:16). Peter defines it as men writing "from God as they were carried along by the Holy Spirit" (2 Peter 1:21).

The inspiration of the Scriptures goes far beyond God-given human genius or charisma. It's more than great thoughts or events which inspire the reader or hearer. The very words of Scripture are true; not just parts, but the whole.

Sometimes the Lord dictated the exact words to be recorded for all time (Ex. 34:27-29). Other times, He allowed His prophets' unique personalities to be reflected in their writings. Many authors acknowledged collecting oral testimonies or consulting written records. Some dictated to secretaries, while others wrote longhand. But in any case, God guarantees that He inspired and authored what Moses and the other Bible prophets recorded.

The following sketch of each Old Testament author and his writings takes them in chronological order, beginning with the earliest. For a fuller discussion about the historical background and contents of each Bible book, consult a Bible dictionary or introductory notes in a study/reference Bible. All dates in this chapter are B.C., before Christ, unless otherwise noted.

Moses—The Great Lawgiver

Jesus and many other Bible authors agree that Moses began the Bible about 1,450 years before Christ, writing at God's command (Luke 24:27; 2 Chron. 35:6). Moses penned the first five Bible books (Gen., Ex., Lev., Num., and Deut.) plus Psalm 90 and the Book of Job between 1445 and 1405 B.C.

Moses' 229 chapters comprise about one fourth of the Old Testament or one fifth of the whole Bible. His first five books are considered a unit known as the *Law, Pentateuch* (Greek for "five books"), or *Torah* (Hebrew for "law").

Part of the Pentateuch was written directly by God. "When the Lord finished speaking to Moses on Mount Sinai, he gave him the two tablets of the Testimony, the tablets of stone inscribed by the finger of God. . . . The tablets were the work of God; the writing was the writing of God, engraved on the tablets" (Ex. 31:18; 32:16).

But most of the Torah was written by Moses, who spent 40 days on Mount Sinai* inscribing God's words for the Hebrews. "Moses then wrote down everything the Lord had said" (Ex. 24:4). Moses claimed to be consciously writing words he received directly from God.

Moses and the other Old Testament prophets wrote in Hebrew, a language whose letters are written from right to left. Hebrew books are read from back to front. Originally Hebrew was written as an unbroken succession of letters with no spaces between words. Nor were there any vowels, only consonants. But this is no problem to those who know the language, as modern Hebrew newspapers are still printed this way.

With no neuter gender (everything is male or female) and a limited vocabulary (concrete nouns conjure up a pool of meanings), Hebrew is a very graphic language, well suited for the biography, history, and poetry found in the Old Testament.

Ancient authors such as Moses used whatever smooth surface was available—stones, clay tablets, but mainly parch-

---

*To locate places mentioned in this book see atlases listed in Appendix B (see p. 8) on page 151.

ment—dried and polished skins of calves or sheep. Pen-and-ink writing was done on scrolls—long strips of parchment sewn together and wound around poles like window shades. The average scroll was between 20 and 35 feet in length, though the longest one discovered was 144 feet. Writing was usually done only on one side so it would be protected as the scroll was rolled from one hand to the other.

Because he angrily broke the first set of commandment tablets when he saw the Hebrews worshiping a golden calf, Moses had to ascend the mount for a replay. Nothing was left to chance or Moses' memory. God dictated His law records to His Hebrew scribe:

> Then the Lord said to Moses, "Write down these words, for in accordance with these words I have made a covenant with you and with Israel." Moses was there with the Lord forty days and forty nights without eating bread or drinking water. And he wrote on the tablets the words of the covenant—the Ten Commandments. When Moses came down from Mount Sinai with the two tablets of the Testimony in his hands, he was not aware that his face was radiant because he had spoken with the Lord (Ex. 34:27-29).

Moses didn't aspire to his leadership role over the Hebrew nation. Nor did he set out to found a new religion. When first approached by God for the task, octogenarian Moses offered five excuses as to why he could not be a spokesman for God or the Hebrews (Ex. 3–4). Moses was content to continue herding sheep, his occupation for the preceding 40 years.

Moses had been born under a death sentence to Levitical Hebrew slaves in Egypt, but through his family's ingenuity and providential protection, Moses was raised as a prince in the Pharaoh's family. His name means "son of water," reminiscent of his rescue from the Nile by the Pharaoh's daughter. After receiving the best education available in his world, Moses at age 40 sided with his Hebrew ancestry, killed an

Egyptian taskmaster, and fled for his life to the wilderness of Midian, where God called him 40 years later at a burning bush. Moses needed training as both a prince and a pauper for his 40-year term as the Hebrews' headmaster.

Moses never claimed originality for his words or writings—rather he spoke and wrote only what he received directly from God. The divine authority behind Moses' message was obvious, confirmed by miracles. Those who challenged him were stricken with leprosy or swallowed alive by the earth (Deut. 34:10-11; Num. 12:6-10; 16:28-35). Throughout the rest of Bible history, the Pentateuch is the basis for Jewish faith and life. Psalms quote from it extensively, and it is the basis for the prophets' messages. Jesus said about Moses' writings, "Do not think that I have come to abolish the Law or the Prophets; I have not come to abolish them but to fulfill them" (Matt. 5:17).

What Moses Wrote

In Genesis, Moses records God's creation of the universe, mankind's fall into sin, a worldwide flood, and scattering of the nations from Babel. Moses' world history then focuses on the Hebrew race through its first four generations (Abraham, Isaac, Jacob, and Joseph) and their migration from Chaldea through Canaan to Egypt.

Job probably lived during the time of the Hebrew patriarchs (between 2200 and 1400) because he lived so long (140 years beyond his suffering as an adult with 10 grown children). Since he served as priest for his extended family, Job lived before the Levites were appointed at Mount Sinai about 1445. The Book of Job doesn't mention its author, but the Talmud, the authoritative book of Jewish tradition, says Moses wrote it. Job's home (Uz) was near Midian, where Moses lived for 40 years, and was also part of the wilderness which Moses trekked with the Israelites for another 40 years.

Most of Moses' writings are narrative in nature, a retelling of history. The books of Joshua through Esther will later follow this format. But in the Book of Job, Moses uses an altogether different literary style—Hebrew poetry—in which *thoughts* are "rhymed." The Books of Psalms and Song of Solomon follow this format. It's interesting that the prophetic books (Isaiah through Malachi) are a combination of narrative and poetry.

The Book of Exodus records the Hebrews' multiplication into a multitude of millions during their 400 years in Egypt and God's preparation of Moses as their deliverer. After 10 plagues and the first Passover, Moses led the Hebrew mob through the Red Sea to Mount Sinai, where God gave His Law. After issuing hundreds of commands covering the moral, civil, and ceremonial lives of His people, God gave detailed directions for building the tabernacle, a portable worship center.

While camped at Mount Sinai, the Hebrew tribe of Levi was selected to serve as the priests, representing the other Israelites before the Lord. Leviticus is their training manual on how to offer five kinds of sacrifices for sin and gratitude. They were also taught how to conduct seven annual feasts to commemorate important events in Hebrew history.

After being taught God's ways and organized to move about 100 miles from Sinai to Canaan, the newly formed Hebrew nation sent spies into their Promised Land. Forty days of unbelief toward God resulted in 40 years in the wilderness south of the Dead Sea. Still led by a century-plus-old Moses, the second Hebrew generation conquered lands east of the Jordan River. The Book of Numbers chronicles these 40 wilderness years between Sinai and Moab.

In Deuteronomy 1–33, Moses reviews the Hebrews' history from Egypt to the present, encouraging them to be faithful to their faithful God. After restating God's laws and extracting a promise from the Hebrews to always love and obey God, Moses died at age 120 in Moab, east of the Jordan River. Though God buried Moses' body in an unmarked grave, He took his spirit to heaven. Moses appeared on earth again about 1400 years later (Luke 9:30)! The Hebrews mourned 30 days for their beloved leader, of whom Joshua says:

Since then, no prophet has risen in Israel like Moses, whom the Lord knew face to face, who did all those miraculous signs and wonders the Lord sent him to do in Egypt—to Pharaoh and to all his officials and to his whole land. For no one has ever shown the mighty power or performed the awesome deeds that Moses did in the sight of all Israel (Deut. 34:10-12).

Probably late in life, Moses also wrote Psalm 90, a moving prayer for wise use of time based on the brevity of human life.

Sacred from the Start

Moses' writings were immediately considered to be from God and stored in the most holy place of the Hebrews' worship center, the sacred ark of the covenant (Deut. 31:24-26). Later they were transferred to the temple in Jerusalem.

In the twentieth century some liberal critics challenged Moses' single authorship of the Pentateuch, espousing instead a theory that it was a compilation of many unknown authors and editors, not finished until the seventh century. But overwhelming evidence and 3500 years of tradition confirm it was written within 50 years of the Exodus by Moses, as the Scriptures clearly claim.

Archaeological finds, such as the Moabite Stone, Ras Shamra Tablets, and Siloam Inscriptions, to select a few from hundreds, have verified that writing was common before Moses' time. Libraries of thousands of inscribed and baked clay tablets have been unearthed in the Tigris-Euphrates Valley, the Tel el-Amarna collection being one of the most famous.

Is it more than a coincidence that the oldest examples of alphabetic writing on stone have been discovered in the region of Mt. Sinai dating from about 1500, the very time and place where Moses began to write the Bible? It's also interesting that the oldest evidences of civilization have been unearthed in the Mesopotamian Valley, where Moses said God began mankind (Gen. 2).

Moses personally experienced most of the events about which he wrote (Ex. 2–Deut. 33). Moses may have received his knowledge of events preceding his lifetime (Gen. 1–Ex. 1) as historical records written by others, oral tradition, or directly from God. In any event, God guarantees the accuracy of what Moses recorded (2 Peter 1:20-21).

Having predicted God would raise up a line of prophets like himself, Moses began a chain of Old Testament written revelation from God that continued for about a thousand years (from 1400 to 400; Deut. 18:15-22). See Chart 3 for a listing of the Old Testament authors in chronological order with the writings and occupations of each.

THE OLD TESTAMENT AUTHORS
(Chart 3)

AUTHOR	WRITINGS	# CHAP.	OCCUPATION(S)
Moses	Genesis 1–Deuteronomy 33	186	prince, shepherd,
	Psalm 90	1	Hebrew national
	Job	42	leader
Joshua	Deuteronomy 34	1	military commander,
	Joshua 1:1–24:28	24	scout, apprentice, Hebrew national leader
Eleazar	Joshua 24:29-32	4 vv.	high priest, metal worker, census taker
Phinehas	Joshua 24:33	1 v.	high priest, gatekeeper at tabernacle, military chaplain
Samuel	Judges	21	judge, priest,

AUTHOR	WRITINGS	# CHAP.	OCCUPATION(S)
	Ruth	4	prophet, Hebrew
	1 Samuel 1–24	24	national leader
Nathan (with Gad)	1 Samuel 25–2 Samuel 24	31	prophet, king's counselor
Gad (with Nathan)	1 Samuel 25–2 Samuel 24	31	prophet, king's counselor
David	Psalms 2–9; 11–32; 34–41; 51–65; 68–70; 86; 95; 101; 103; 108–110; 122; 124; 131; 133; 138–145;	75	shepherd, musician, poet, military hero, king of Judah & Israel
	compiler of Psalms 1–41	?	
Asaph	Psalms 50; 73–83, maybe compiler of Psalms 1–41	12	priest, prophet, temple musician, worship leader
Korah's descendants Assir Elkanah Abiasaph Assir Tahath Uriel Uzziah Shaul	Psalms 42; 44–49; 84; 85; 87	10	priests, composers, singers
Ethan	Psalm 89	1	wise man
Heman	Psalm 88	1	wise man

AUTHOR	WRITINGS	# CHAP.	OCCUPATION(S)
Solomon	Song of Solomon Proverbs 1–29 Psalms 72; 127 Ecclesiastes	8 29 2 12	King of Israel, world's wisest man, poet, musician, botanist, zoologist, statesman
Agur	Proverbs 30	1	wise man
Lemuel	Proverbs 31	1	Arabian prince?
Ahijah	parts of Kings & Chronicles	?	prophet
Iddo	parts of Kings & Chronicles, genealogies of Hebrew kings	?	prophet, Levite, seer
Shemaiah	parts of Kings & Chronicles, genealogies of Hebrew kings	?	prophet
Jehu	parts of Kings & Chronicles	?	prophet
Obadiah	Obadiah	1	prophet, palace servant?
Joel	Joel	3	prophet
Jonah	Jonah	4	prophet
Amos	Amos	9	herdsman, farmer, prophet
Hosea	Hosea	14	farmer?, baker?, prophet
Micah	Micah	7	farmer, prophet
Isaiah	Isaiah	66	prophet

AUTHOR	WRITINGS	# CHAP.	OCCUPATION(S)
Hezekiah	compiler/editor of Proverbs 30 and maybe Psalms 42–89	?	king, civil engineer
Nahum	Nahum	3	prophet
Zephaniah	Zephaniah	3	prophet
Jeremiah	1 Kings 1–2 Kings 24 Jeremiah Lamentations	46 52 5	priest, prophet
Baruch	Jeremiah 52:31-34	4 vv.	scribe, secretary
Habakkuk	Habakkuk	3	musician, prophet, priest?
Daniel	Daniel	12	wise man, prophet, Babylonian & Persian official, Jewish noble
Ezekiel	Ezekiel	48	priest, prophet
Haggai	Haggai	2	prophet
Zechariah	Zechariah	14	priest, prophet
Mordecai	Esther	10	Jewish lobbyist, Persian government official
Ezra	1 and 2 Chronicles Ezra Nehemiah compiler-editor of Psalms 90–150	65 10 13 61	priest, scribe, Bible teacher, revival leader

AUTHOR	WRITINGS	# CHAP.	OCCUPATION(S)
Nehemiah	Nehemiah 1:1–7:5; 11:27–12:43; 13:4-31	9	cupbearer to Persian king, governor of Judah and Jerusalem
Malachi	Malachi	4	prophet
Anonymous	2 Kings 25	1	
	Psalms 1; 10; 33; 43; 66; 67; 71; 91–94; 96–100; 102; 104–107; 111–121; 123; 125; 126; 128–130; 132; 134–137; 146–150	48	

Note: Because of overlaps between authors and editors as well as uncertainty about authorship of some portions, the number of chapters adds up to more than the 929 in the Old Testament.

3

From the Pasture to the Palace

The Old Testament Writers, Part 2

God told Joshua, Moses' successor:

> Be strong and very courageous. Be careful to obey all
> the law my servant Moses gave you; do not turn from it
> to the right or to the left, that you may be successful
> wherever you go. Do not let this Book of the Law
> depart from your mouth; meditate on it day and night,
> so that you may be careful to do everything written in
> it. Then you will be prosperous and successful (Joshua
> 1:7-8).

Moses' first five books were viewed as one unit and were
to be the authoritative guide for God's people.

Joshua, whose name means "Jehovah is salvation," is first
mentioned in Scripture as the victorious commander of the
Hebrews in their first battle after being freed from Egypt
(Ex. 17:8-16). When Moses twice ascended Sinai to receive
God's Law, Joshua accompanied him part way and waited
for him on the mountain (Ex. 24:13; 32:17). After Israel's sin

with the golden calf, Moses appointed Joshua in charge of guarding the sacred tabernacle.

Joshua was honored with Caleb for his faith as one of the two scouts of Canaan who believed the Lord (Num. 14:24, 30). He had already risen to leadership over his large Hebrew tribe of Ephraim (Num. 13:3, 8). Born in Egypt, Joshua experienced God's miracles associated with the Exodus, God's revelation at Mount Sinai, and the Hebrews' 40 years in the wilderness.

Since Joshua served as Moses' aide since his youth (Num. 11:28) and had become Moses' intimate friend, it seemed fitting when God appointed Joshua to replace Moses as the Hebrews' leader. The Book of Joshua records how Commander Joshua led the Hebrews to conquer Canaan, their Promised Land, about 1400 and divide it among the 12 Hebrew tribes.

Near the end of his life (about 1380), "Joshua recorded these things in the Book of the Law of God" (Joshua 24:26). Joshua added his sacred writings to the *book* of Moses (Gen.–Deut. together), probably beginning with the record of Moses' death (Deut. 34). Jewish scholars sometimes refer to the Books of Genesis–Joshua as a unit called the *hexateuch* (Greek for "six books").

In his 25 chapters (Deut. 34–Josh. 24), Joshua eulogizes his old friend and leader, calling Moses "the servant of the Lord" and "the man of God," terms the humble leader had not previously used for himself. Because Moses and Joshua, the first two leaders of the Hebrews after their Exodus from Egypt, ruled under God's direction, their era is called a theocracy ("rule by God"). Joshua died in Ephraim of old age.

Eleazar and Phinehas—Priestly Postscripters

Though the Talmud states Joshua wrote the book bearing his name, it also says the last five verses of the book were written by two others. Eleazar, Moses' nephew (third son of his brother Aaron), appended Joshua's death notice (Joshua 24:29-32). Moses inaugurated Eleazar as the Hebrews' high priest just before Aaron's death about 1406. Eleazar, whose name means "God has helped," helped Moses take a census of the Hebrews, took part in Joshua's inauguration, and helped him divide Canaan among the Hebrew tribes. The Jewish historian Josephus says Eleazar and Joshua both died about 25 years after Moses, who died in 1405. Eleazar and his priestly descendants were highly commended servants of God.

Eleazar's son Phinehas ("the Nubian") added the notice about his father's death (Joshua 24:33). In his first appearance in Scripture, Phinehas' bold zeal for God stopped a plague that was destroying the Hebrew nation, for which God highly praised him and promised the Hebrew priesthood would remain in his family (Num. 25:7-13).

God later said, "[The Hebrews] provoked the Lord to anger by their wicked deeds, and a plague broke out among them. But Phinehas stood up and intervened, and the plague was checked. This was credited to him as righteousness for endless generations to come" (Ps. 106:29-31).

Phinehas was the first since Abraham to receive such a divine accolade (Gen. 15:6). Phinehas' descendants held the Hebrew priesthood until Jerusalem and the temple were destroyed in A.D. 70.

Phinehas served as a military chaplain and succeeded his father as the Hebrew high priest (Num. 31:6). Phinehas also served as the chief of the Korahites, a group of Levites called gatekeepers, responsible to guard the tabernacle and later the temple in Jerusalem. When Joshua divided Canaan, Phinehas was awarded a hill after on Mount Ephraim. Phinehas' tomb near Nablus is revered by both Jews and Samaritans. Authoring one verse gives Phinehas the distinction of writing the least amount of the Bible.

The next Scripture writer is Samuel, to whom the Talmud ascribes two Bible books: Judges–Ruth and Samuel (both later divided into two books). Altogether, Samuel produced 49 chapters of sacred history.

Samuel—The Public Servant

Samuel ("asked of God") was born in answer to his mother's fervent prayers and dedicated to live and serve the Lord at the tabernacle from childhood (1 Sam. 1:11, 24-28). While an apprentice to the high priest, Samuel was audibly called by God to serve as Israel's next prophet and spiritual leader (1 Sam. 3:1-21). All of his predictions were exactly fulfilled as stated.

After proclaiming a national day of repentance and prayer in response to Israel's idolatry and Philistia's oppression, Samuel was recognized as the Hebrews' next judge. God routed the enemy, and Samuel became Israel's political and spiritual leader (1 Sam. 7:3-12).

In response to the people's demands and God's accession, Samuel inaugurated Saul as the first Hebrew king. Continuing as God's faithful spokesman, Samuel three times reproved King Saul's sins. Each time the king rationalized his errant behavior and was finally rejected by God as king in lieu of David. Samuel anointed David as the next king and befriended him in the face of their common enemy, jealous and murderous Saul.

Though the Hebrews rejected Samuel as their political leader for a king, no one could point out any fault in Samuel's life. God continued to authenticate His prophet through miracles (1 Sam. 12:1-5, 16-18). There was no bitterness or desire for revenge in Samuel. Rather, he said:

> For the sake of His great name the Lord will not reject His people, because the Lord was pleased to make you His own. As for me, far be it from me that I should sin against the Lord by failing to pray for you. And I will teach you the way that is good and right. But be sure to fear the Lord and serve Him faithfully with all your heart; consider what great things He has done for you (1 Sam. 12:22-24).

Samuel stands as an outstanding example of a public servant's unswerving devotion to God and His people.

Great mourning followed Samuel's death in about 1017. From the hill of his tomb above Gibeon, Jerusalem can be seen.

In his Book of Judges, Samuel records a period in Israel's history when, for the most part, each Hebrew did whatever was right in his own eyes (Judges 21:25). Seven times the Hebrews experienced a national cycle of iniquity, indention to a foreign power, intercession to God, and independence gained through a deliverer who would rule temporarily as a judge. Since Judges spans 330 years of history (about 1380–1050), Samuel may have compiled and edited historical accounts of predecessors.

During the dark era of the Judges, the Book of Ruth details how a Moabite widow, Ruth, accompanied and cared for her Hebrew mother-in-law Naomi. Her second marriage to Boaz placed her in the Messiah's family tree by becoming the great grandmother of King David of Israel. Josephus records that the Book of Ruth was originally an appendix to the Book of Judges (*Against Apion, 1:8*).

In 1 Samuel 1–24, Samuel adds his personal history to the growing volume of Scripture. As the last of 14 Hebrew judges and anointer of their first two kings, Samuel is the transition link from theocracy to monarchy in the Hebrew nation.

Nathan and Gad—The Prophet-Historians

Nathan and Gad completed the histories of Saul and David, starting with Samuel's death (1 Sam. 25:1). The author of 1 Chronicles ascribes to Nathan and Gad the recording of the lives of David and Solomon (1 Chron. 29:29-30; 2 Chron. 9:29). Together these two prophets produced 31 chapters of Scripture.

Nathan ("God has given") was a key prophet of God during the 80 years of David's and Solomon's reigns (1010–930). He instructed David that he would not be allowed to build God's temple in Jerusalem; instead God would make an everlasting "house" of David's descendants (2 Sam. 7).

To Nathan fell the delicate task of confronting David about his sin with Bathsheba and arranged murder of her husband Uriah. God had given David the better part of a year to repent. The prophet's cleverly-crafted parable of a rich man who stole and slaughtered a poor neighbor's pet lamb slipped the truth past David's defenses, setting him up to receive God's rebuke (2 Sam. 12:1-15). He continued as the king's friend and counselor, helping David reorganize the Levitical worship leaders for the temple Solomon would build in Jerusalem.

At Solomon's birth to David and Bathsheba, Nathan brought presents and a special nickname from God for the baby to show that God held no grudge against the now-married couple (2 Sam. 12:24-25). Later Nathan secured Solomon's kingship and participated in his inauguration in 970 (1 Kings 1:8-45). Two of his sons served King Solomon (1 Kings 4:5). Nathan's grave is near Hebron.

Gad ("good fortune") joined David as his counselor when the king-to-be was a fugitive hiding in a cave from King Saul (2 Sam. 22:5). David safely moved his forces at the prophet's advice.

When David became king in 1010, Gad continued as the king's seer throughout his 40-year reign. As God's spokesman, he presented David with a choice of judgments for pridefully counting his subjects (2 Sam. 24:11-19). Gad also worked with David and Nathan to prearrange musical services for Solomon's temple (2 Chron. 29:25).

First Samuel 25–31 begins with the account of Samuel's death and continues through King Saul's reign to his suicide. In 2 Samuel the prophetic pair record David's kingship, including his meteoric rise to fame (chaps. 1–10), sin with Bathsheba (chaps. 11–12), and the tragic consequences of his forgiven sin (chaps. 13–24).

The Book of the Acts of Solomon, source material for Ezra in writing the Books of 1 and 2 Chronicles, may refer to Nathan's and Gad's accounts of Solomon's life.

David—The Man After God's Own Heart

Israel's most famous king, David ("beloved" or "chief"), was born in Bethlehem, Judah, the youngest of Jesse's eight sons. During his boyhood years as a shepherd, he used his long hours of solitude to develop his musical composition and harp performance skills (1 Sam. 16:18, 23).

David's poetical songs (psalms) were inspired by his meditation on the Bible, which at that time would have contained at least the Pentateuch, and more likely, the Hexateuch. Many of his writings spring from this youthful era, the most notable being Psalm 23, the "Shepherd Psalm."

> The Lord is my shepherd, I shall not be in want. He makes me lie down in green pastures, He leads me beside quiet waters, He restores my soul. He guides me in paths of righteousness for His name's sake. Even though I walk through the valley of the shadow of death, I will fear no evil, for you are with me; your rod and your staff, they comfort me. You prepare a table before me in the presence of my enemies. You anoint my head with oil; my cup overflows. Surely goodness and love will follow me all the days of my life, and I will dwell in the house of the Lord forever (Ps. 23:1-6).

David's youthful courage is displayed in his killing a lion and a bear to defend his sheep (1 Sam. 17:34-36). While shepherding, David was summoned from his flock to be anointed by Samuel as the second king of the Hebrew nation, a position he wouldn't occupy until many years later.

Periodically King Saul called David to play and sing to dispel Saul's troublesome evil spirits. But the jealous king made many attempts on David's life and spent his final years pursuing David with his army. Most of David's Psalms come from his crucible of suffering during these years before he replaced Saul on Israel's throne. His writings carry the dual strains of desiring God to take swifter action against his persecutors, and gratitude and confidence for what God was doing on his behalf. David's exemplary attitude is seen in his writings as well as his sparing Saul's life on at least two occasions.

After Saul's death, David continued to compose while he served as Israel's king. Some Psalms commemorate great successes in the king's career, such as capturing Jerusalem and making it his capital, expanding Israel's boundaries to the largest ever, and bringing the sacred ark of the covenant to a permanent worship center in Jerusalem.

Other Psalms reflect David's grief over his adultery (32, 51), nationwide famine and pestilence, and rebellion by his son Absalom.

David's selfless devotion to God is clearly seen in his many years of gathering materials and making arrangements for the temple his successor would build. Many Psalms were specifically written for a choir to sing at worship services. What a contrast to Saul, who only made life hard for his successor.

Between 1050 and 970, David penned 75 Psalms (2–9; 11–32; 34–41; 51–65; 68–70; 86; 95; 101; 103; 108–110; 122; 124; 131; 133; 138–145). David's authorship of 73 Psalms is noted in the ancient superscriptions (headings) attached to them, while the New Testament ascribes two additional seemingly anonymous Psalms to him (2 and 95; see Acts 4:25 and Heb. 4:7). Altogether, David wrote half of the Book of Psalms. Many superscriptions not only ascribe authorship, but also the historical occasion of the Psalm. It's interesting that the New Testament introduces what David wrote with the prayer, "You spoke by the Holy Spirit through the mouth of your servant, our father David" (Acts 4:25).

Centuries later, God gave David His highest commendation, saying " 'I have found David son of Jesse a man after my own heart; he will do everything I want him to do.' From this man's descendants God has brought to Israel the Saviour Jesus, as He promised" (Acts 13:22-23). As a prominent member of the Hebrew tribe of Judah, David is a key link in Jesus' genealogy.

After ruling the Hebrews for 40 years, David died at age 70 in 970 and was given a royal burial in Jerusalem.

Asaph to Heman—The Other Psalmists
Asaph, appointed by David to lead the sacred temple choirs (1 Chron. 16:5) sometime between 1000 and 970, com-

posed 12 Psalms (50, 73–83). Asaph may also have collected the majority of David's Psalms and a few by others into Book 1 of the Psalms (Pss. 1–41). His ministry as poet, prophet, and musician continued into Solomon's reign (2 Chron. 29:30). His unnamed and unnumbered sons were also temple choristers (1 Chron. 25:1-2). As late as Nehemiah's time 550 years later, David's and Asaph's directions for temple praise services were still being followed (Neh. 12:46).

Ten Psalms (42; 44–49; 84; 85; 87) are ascribed to the "sons" or male descendants of Korah in the tribe of Levi, which may have included Assir, Elkanah, Ebiasaph, Tahath, Uriel, Uzziah, and Shaul (1 Chron. 6:22-24, 31-38). Korah, a cousin and contemporary of Moses, was a gate guard at the tabernacle (1 Chron. 9:17-21). Though he and some of his family were swallowed up by the earth for leading a rebellion against Moses and Aaron, Korah's sons were spared to form a guild of composers and singers who ministered at the tabernacle and later the temple (Num. 26:9-11).

A grandson of the prophet Samuel and renowned as a seer, Heman wrote Psalm 88, while Ethan authored Psalm 89 (1 Chron. 6:33; 2 Chron. 35:15). Both of these Levites played bronze cymbals and were leaders of the temple music appointed by David (1 Chron. 15:19).

The Psalms were written to be sung to the accompaniment of stringed instruments at the tabernacle and later at the temple in Jerusalem. The gradual collection was originally known as the Book of Praises. Smaller anthologies of Psalms were collected first, some according to author, such as David's and Asaph's (Ps. 72:20; 2 Chron. 29:30.). Others were arranged by topic, such as the "Pilgrim" Psalms (120–134) or "Hallelujah" Psalms (145–150). Eventually, the Psalms were organized into five sub-books, the end of each marked by a doxology (an ascription of praise to God). Book 1 (Pss. 1–41) is mainly David's and may have been assembled by him or his worship leader, Asaph. The reformer king Hezekiah may have added books 2 (42–72) and 3 (73–89) around 710, while the scribe and priest Ezra may have compiled books 4 (90–106) and 5 (107–150) around 430 (2 Chron. 29:30).

Though the authors of Psalms span about 500 years, from Moses (Ps. 90, about 1450) to the Jews' Babylonian Exile (Ps. 137, about 500) the topics included range far further, from the Creation to the Christ and His future kingdom.

4

From the City and the Country

The Old Testament Writers, Part 3

Soon after his birth to Bathsheba, Solomon received presents and a special name Jedidiah ("beloved of Jehovah") from God. Solomon was raised by King David, the man after God's own heart, and developed a love for God and the Scriptures.

After Solomon's coronation as Israel's third king, God said to him, "Ask for whatever you want me to give you."

Solomon answered:

"Your servant is here among the people you have chosen, a great people, too numerous to count or number. So give your servant a discerning heart to govern your people and to distinguish between right and wrong. For who is able to govern this great people of yours?" [God was pleased with the new king's request, saying,] "I will do what you have asked. I will give you a wise and discerning heart, so that there will never have been anyone like you, nor will there ever be. Moreover, I will give you what you have not asked for—both riches and honor—so that in your lifetime you will have no equal among kings" (1 Kings 3:8-9, 12-13).

Solomon indeed became world renowned for his wealth and wisdom:

He spoke three thousand proverbs and his songs numbered a thousand and five. He described plant life, from the cedar of Lebanon to the hyssop that grows out of walls. He also taught about animals and birds, reptiles and fish. Men of all nations came to listen to Solomon's wisdom, sent by all the kings of the world, who had heard of his wisdom (1 Kings 4:32-34).

Nine hundred and fifteen of Solomon's 3,000 wise sayings are recorded in Proverbs 1–29 for the purpose of the reader (originally his son Rehoboam) "attaining wisdom and discipline; for understanding words of insight; for acquiring a disciplined and prudent life, doing what is right and just and fair; for giving prudence to the simple, knowledge and discretion to the young" (Prov. 1:2-4). Chapters 25–29 were collected and copied in the time of King Hezekiah (ca. 700 B.C.; Prov. 25:1).

After the Queen of Sheba traveled 1,200 miles to consult Solomon and see firsthand the splendor of his kingdom, she exclaimed:

The report I heard in my own country about your achievements and your wisdom is true. But I did not believe these things until I came and saw with my own eyes. Indeed, not even half was told me; in wisdom and wealth you have far exceeded the report I heard (1 Kings 10:6-7).

Enjoying an era of world peace, Solomon established worldwide manufacturing and trading enterprises to become Israel's first great commercial king. To cement peace treaties with the surrounding nations, Solomon broke God's law when he married many foreign women and later joined them in idol worship. From his younger years, the king describes the joys of married love with one of his wives in the Song of Solomon.

Solomon's crowning achievement was building God a magnificent temple in Jerusalem, Israel. Seven years in construction as a multi-national project, it remained the Hebrew's worship shrine for almost 400 years. During the 14-day dedication ceremony, Solomon knelt before the Lord and his subjects, praying aloud one of the Bible's longest recorded prayers. The tender heart of the king toward God is felt in this excerpt:

And forgive your people, who have sinned against you; forgive all the offenses they have committed against you, and cause their conquerors to show them mercy; for they are your people and your inheritance, whom you brought out of Egypt, out of that iron-smelting furnace. May your eyes be open to your servant's plea and to the plea of your people Israel, and may you listen to them whenever they cry out to you. For you singled them out from all the nations of the world to be your own inheritance, just as you declared through your servant Moses when you, O Sovereign Lord, brought our fathers out of Egypt (1 Kings 8:50-53).

He then blessed his people, saying:

Praise be to the Lord, who has given rest to His people Israel just as He promised. Not one word has failed of all the good promises He gave through His servant Moses. May the Lord our God be with us as He was with our fathers; may He never leave us nor forsake us. May he turn our hearts to Him, to walk in all His ways and to keep the commands, decrees and regulations He gave our fathers. And may these words of mine, which I have prayed before the Lord, be near to the Lord our God day and night, that He may uphold the cause of

His servant and the cause of His people Israel according to each day's need, so that all the peoples of the earth may know that the Lord is God and that there is no other. But your hearts must be fully committed to the Lord our God, to live by His decrees and obey His commands, as at this time (1 Kings 8:56-61).

Solomon's confidence was not in what he could achieve, as he clarifies in Psalm 127:1, "Unless the Lord builds the house, its builders labor in vain. Unless the Lord watches over the city, the watchmen stand guard in vain."

Later in life, influenced by his pagan wives, Solomon drifted from his spiritual moorings. Gleaning from his experiences of trying to find fulfillment in pleasure, wealth, work, friends, popularity, religion, marriage, children, and status, in the Book of Ecclesiastes Solomon declared them all to be empty apart from a relationship with God. The aged king concluded the key to a satisfying life is to, "Fear God, and keep His commandments; for this is the whole duty of man" (Ecc. 12:13).

Between 970 and 930 B.C. Solomon wrote the Song of Solomon, Proverbs 1–29, Ecclesiastes, and Psalms 72 and 127: a total of 51 Bible chapters.

The official record of the life of Solomon in 1 Kings and 2 Chronicles was written by others, including Jeremiah and Ezra, who are discussed later.

Agur and Lemuel—Proverbial Completers

Little is known of two additional proverbialists. Agur ("gathered") is credited with chapter 30 and Lemuel ("belonging to God") with chapter 31. Both lived in Massa, an unidentified location, perhaps in Arabia.

Lemuel was king of Massa (alternate reading for "oracle" in 31:1) and thus perhaps was a north Arabian prince. Some ancient rabbis (Jewish teachers) identify Lemuel with Solomon. If this is the case, Bathsheba actually originated a Bible chapter, since Lemuel's mother taught him what he recorded in Proverbs 31.

Ahijah and Company—The Kings' Chroniclers

More additions to the Books of Kings and Chronicles (originally one book each) were written at this time. Among the mentioned chroniclers, whose accounts would later be incorporated by Jeremiah and Ezra, are Ahijah, Iddo, Shemaiah, and Jehu.

Ahijah ("brother of Jehovah") lived in Shiloh, Israel, ancient home of the Hebrew tabernacle before Solomon built the temple in Jerusalem. About 940, 10 years before the fact, Ahijah predicted that he would head the secession of 10 tribes from the Hebrew union (1 Kings 11:31-39). After Solomon's son Rehoboam split the Hebrew kingdom, Ahijah continued to minister in Israel, the Northern Kingdom. About 915 Ahijah foretold the immediate death of King Jeroboam's son and the subsequent captivity of the nation of Israel (1 Kings 14:6-16). Ahijah also contributed a record of the events of Solomon's reign (2 Chron. 9:29).

Iddo, from the tribe of Levi, prophesied in Judah, the Hebrew Southern Kingdom. He wrote chronicles of the lives of King Jeroboam of Israel and Judean kings Solomon, Rehoboam, and Abijah (Rehoboam's successor). Iddo, along with Shemaiah, is credited with some of the extensive genealogical records used in Kings and Chronicles. He was also known for his visions as a seer (2 Chron. 9:29; 12:15; 13:22).

Shemaiah ("Jehovah has heard") kept Rehoboam and 180,000 Judean troops from attacking Jeroboam and the 10 Hebrew tribes who had just seceded (1 Kings 12:22–24). Known as "the man of God," Shemaiah delivered the exact words he had received from the Lord. In obeying Shemaiah's words, Rehoboam and his men "obeyed the words of the Lord" (2 Chron. 11:2-4). Because Rehoboam repented on a later occasion after hearing Shemaiah's heaven-sent message, Judah was spared complete destruction by King Shishak of Egypt (2 Chron. 12:5-7). Shemaiah coauthored genealogies with the prophet Iddo.

Jehu ("Jehovah is He") was a Judean prophet who ministered in both Hebrew kingdoms over a period of about 30 years (879–850). Because "the word of the Lord came through the prophet Jehu," he denounced the extreme wickedness of King Baasha of Israel and predicted the end of his family line (1 Kings 16:1-7).

A generation later Jehu rebuked King Jehoshaphat of Judah for making an unholy alliance with wicked King Ahab of Israel, saying, "Should you help the wicked and love those who hate the Lord? Because of this, the wrath of the Lord is upon you. There is, however, some good in you, for you have rid the land of the Asherah poles and have set your heart on seeking God" (2 Chron. 19:2-3). As a result of Jehu's ministry, "Jehoshaphat lived in Jerusalem, and he went out again among the people from Beersheba to the hill country of Ephraim and turned them back to the Lord, the God of their fathers" (19:4).

The Last Seventeen
The last 17 Old Testament prophetic books were all penned after Solomon's son Rehoboam split the Hebrew kingdom in 930. All are named for their human authors except Lamentations, Jeremiah's second prophetic book. Eleven of these men and their books came before Babylonia conquered Judah, the Hebrew Southern Kingdom, in 606. Three prophetic books were produced during the Babylonian Exile, and three after.

Prophets are discussed in the order of their appearance, starting with the earliest. See Chart 3 on page 26 for a chronological listing of all the Old Testament writers.

The nature of the writing changes now from historical to hortatory. These remaining 16 Old Testament authors were change agents more than chroniclers. Each brought God's laws to bear on his or another society. Stories now give way to sermons as the prophets call their generations back to God's standards and spell out the consequences of not heeding.

Obadiah—The Last Word to Edom
Obadiah ("servant of Jehovah") is probably a "commoner" because no mention is made of his ancestry. Of thirteen Old

Testament men sharing the name, Obadiah the prophet may
have been a palace servant for King Ahab and protected
other prophets of God (1 Kings 18:3). If so, he lived in
Israel, the Hebrew Northern Kingdom, after the split into
two rival kingdoms.

Obadiah predicted the complete obliteration of Edom, descendants of Esau, (twin brother of Jacob, whose sons became the 12 tribes of Israel). Their crime? The Edomites
had helped a foreign power attack Judah, the Hebrew Southern Kingdom.

The revolt of Edom against Judah during the reign of
Jehoram (848–841) perfectly fits Obadiah's description
(2 Chron. 21:8-20). He was thus a contemporary of the
prophets Elijah, Elisha, and Joel, as well as rulers Amaziah,
Athaliah, and Joash of Judah.

Petra, capital of Edom cut in the red-rock cliffs, stands
desolate today as a silent testimony of the accuracy of Obadiah's prophecy against it. Writing 21 verses makes Obadiah
author the shortest Old Testament book.

Joel—Elisha's Contemporary

Joel ("Jehovah is God") may have been a priest in Jerusalem, since he makes more than a dozen references to God's
house in his three chapters. Nothing is known of him apart
from his book. His prophecy best fits during the reign of
King Joash of Judah, ministering between 835 and 796. Joel
was contemporary with the Prophet Elisha in Israel to the
north.

After Judah's vegetation was devoured by a plague of lo-
custs, Joel predicted that God's future judgment on the sins
of His people would be far more devastating. But God's goal
in the stern pronouncement is the repentance of His people.
" 'Even now,' declares the Lord, 'return to me with all your
heart, with fasting and weeping and mourning.' Rend your
heart and not your garments. Return to the Lord your God,
for He is gracious and compassionate, slow to anger and
abounding in love, and He relents from sending calamity"
(Joel 2:12-13).

Nowhere in the Old Testament is there an announcement of judgment which is not coupled with God's grace. God takes no delight in the judgment of sin, and would rather have people repent and receive His forgiveness and blessings. But as then, so now. Though the majority will prefer punishment, the faithful few are promised God's blessing (Joel 2:18-32).

Jonah—The Picture of Christ
Jonah ("dove") came from the tribe of Zebulun and lived in Galilee about three miles from Nazareth, Jesus' boyhood town. He was a recognized servant of God in Israel during the reign of King Jeroboam II (782–750), whose actions fulfilled some of Jonah's short-range prophecies (2 Kings 14:23-25). Jonah is also contemporary with Amaziah and Uzziah, kings of Judah.

Jewish tradition says Jonah was the boy the prophet Elijah raised from the dead (1 Kings 17:8-24).

Jonah's most famous mission, however, was traveling to Nineveh, capital of the cruel Assyrian empire, via a great fish, or sea mammal. Centuries later, Jonah's personal experience at sea is quoted by Jesus as the best historical illustration of His coming death, burial, and resurrection (Matt. 12:39-41).

Jonah's short sermon was heeded; the Ninevites repented openly, and God's judgment was averted. The Lord's compassion for the Gentiles (non-Hebrews) in Nineveh illustrate His desire to be known, loved, and obeyed by all the people-groups of the earth.

Amos—The Shepherd-Farmer Prophet
Amos ("burden bearer") lives up to his name in bringing heavy messages to Israel of how far short of God's standards they have fallen. Every social class is weighed and found wanting.

Amos describes his background:

I was neither a prophet nor a prophet's son, but I was a

shepherd, and I also took care of sycamore-fig trees. But the Lord took me from tending the flock and said to me,"Go, prophesy to my people Israel." Now then, hear the word of the Lord. You say, "Do not prophesy against Israel, and stop preaching against the house of Isaac." Therefore this is what the Lord says (Amos 7:14, 17).

Amos' rural background (he grew up in the country 12 miles south of Jerusalem) often crops up (no pun intended) in his writing as he likens the pompous socialite women to cows, and the nation to a basket of rotten fruit, ready to be destroyed.

Ministering at a time of great prosperity in Israel and when the surrounding nations were weak (782–739), Amos' messages fell largely on deaf ears among the self-sufficient, immoral, and unjust Israelites. Being from the rival Hebrew kingdom Judah also helped lower Amos' popularity rating.

Amos' 43-year ministry spanned the reigns of six of the last seven kings of Israel: Jeroboam II, Zechariah, Shallum, Menahem, Pekaniah, and Pekah. These six sovereigns all received the same divine rating as their 12 predecessors: unacceptable to the Almighty. None of the 19 kings of Israel cared about obeying God or furthering their subjects' spiritual welfare.

Hosea—The Harlot's Husband
Hosea's 40-year ministry (755–715) overlapped Amos' to the same nation, Israel, beginning late in the reign of Jeroboam II and extending beyond the last king, Hoshea. Of these six wicked Israeli kings, four were murdered and one was taken hostage by Assyria. Hosea was also contemporary with the Judean prophets Micah and Isaiah and rulers Uzziah, Jotham, Ahaz, and Hezekiah.

Hosea called his nation Israel (seen in reference to "our king," Hosea 7:5) to return to her God, assuring them of His loyal love, which the prophet dramatically illustrated toward his estranged wife. Gomer had deserted Hosea and their three children for a life of harlotry, but her husband's love bought her back and forgave her. Hosea's name ("salvation") means what God offers His people for repentance.

Hosea lived to see the fulfillment of his prophecies when Israel was conquered by Assyria in 722 and the people slain or scattered. For the remainder of the Old Testament, there would now only be one Hebrew kingdom, Judah, in the south.

The last 12 books in English Bibles are called "minor prophets" because of their shorter length compared with the five "major prophets," Isaiah—Daniel. Lamentations in the latter group is quite short, but was originally joined to the Book of Jeremiah. The 12 minor prophets were originally one book in the Hebrew Bible, beginning with Hosea.

Micah—The Country Prophet to the City
Ministering from 740–690 in Judah makes Micah ("who is like Jehovah?") contemporary with the prophets Isaiah and Hosea during the reigns of Jotham, Ahaz, and Hezekiah of Judah. Micah also lived during last two rulers of Israel and beyond their Assyrian conquest.

Micah lived in a Judean agricultural town about 25 miles southwest of Jerusalem on the Philistine border. Similar to Amos' ministry in the north, Micah scrutinized every segment of society and pointed out their moral deficiencies. Perhaps because of his rural environment, Micah had special feeling for the poor and oppressed among his countrymen.

Only the Messiah's appearance could turn such a society's tide. Micah accurately predicted His birth in Bethlehem 700 years ahead of time (5:2)! Micah also accurately predicted the fall of Samaria, capital of Israel (1:6).

The prophet was well aware of the divine source of his message:

The word of the Lord that came to Micah of Moresheth. . . . But as for me, I am filled with power, with the Spirit of the Lord, and with justice and might, to declare to Jacob his transgression, to Israel his sin (Micah 1:1; 3:8).

5

From the Majors to the Minors

The Old Testament Writers, Part 4

Isaiah's large vocabulary and polished poetic style bespeak a high level of education and a distinguished Jewish family background. Married to a prophetess and the father of at least two sons, Isaiah invested a lot of his ministry among the Jewish royalty in Jerusalem. He had contact with five Judean kings: Uzziah, Jotham, Ahaz, Hezekiah, and Manasseh.

Contemporary with Micah and Hosea, Isaiah's ministry to Judah coincided with Assyria's conquest and scattering of Israel. Isaiah prophesied over a period of at least 60 years, from 740 to 680 B.C.

Not only did Isaiah minister the longest of the Old Testament prophets, he also wrote the Bible's longest single-authored book. The 66 chapters of Isaiah are similar in theme to the Bible's 66 books, with the first 39 about God's laws which reveal our sins and their consequences and the last 27 about the Messiah who redeems us from them.

Many of the 306 specific Old Testament prophecies about Christ come from Isaiah. The statistical odds of even a few of them coming true about the same person stagger the imagination. How fitting that Isaiah's name means "the Lord is salvation."

Among Isaiah's immortal passages about the Lord Jesus Christ are:

> For unto us a child is born, to us a son is given, and the government will be on his shoulders. And he will be called Wonderful Counselor, Mighty God, Everlasting Father, Prince of Peace. Of the increase of his government and peace there will be no end. He will reign on David's throne and over his kingdom, establishing and upholding it with justice and righteousness from that time on and forever. The zeal of the Lord Almighty will accomplish this (Isa. 9:6-7).

When Isaiah 53 has been read to people unacquainted with Scripture, they assume it was written by one of Jesus' apostles. They are astounded to learn the words were penned nearly 700 years before Christ came to earth. How many prophecies can you pick out from this famous chapter?

> Who has believed our message and to whom has the arm of the Lord been revealed? He grew up before him like a tender shoot, and like a root out of dry ground. He had no beauty or majesty to attract us to him, nothing in his appearance that we should desire him. He was despised and rejected by men, a man of sorrows, and familiar with suffering. Like one from whom men hide their faces he was despised, and we esteemed him not. Surely he took up our infirmities and carried our sorrows, yet we considered him stricken by God, smitten by him, and afflicted. But he was pierced for our transgressions, he was crushed for our iniquities; the punishment that brought us peace was upon him, and by his wounds we are healed. We all, like sheep, have gone astray, each of us has turned to his own way; and the Lord has laid on him the iniquity of us all. He was

oppressed and afflicted, yet he did not open his mouth; he was led like a lamb to the slaughter, and as a sheep before her shearers is silent, so he did not open his mouth. By oppression and judgment he was taken away. And who can speak of his descendants? For he was cut off from the land of the living; for the transgression of my people he was stricken. He was assigned a grave with the wicked, and with the rich in his death, though he had done no violence, nor was any deceit in his mouth. Yet it was the Lord's will to crush him and cause him to suffer, and though the Lord makes his life a guilt offering, he will see his offspring and prolong his days, and the will of the Lord will prosper in his hand. After the suffering of his soul, he will see the light of life and be satisfied; by his knowledge my righteous servant will justify many, and he will bear their iniquities. Therefore I will give him a portion among the great, and he will divide the spoils with the strong, because he poured out his life unto death, and was numbered with the transgressors. For he bore the sin of many, and made intercession for the transgressors (Isa. 53:1-12).

The Talmud says Isaiah was sawn in two by wicked King Manasseh's command (cf. Heb. 11:37).

Hezekiah—The Royal Editor
Godly King Hezekiah of Judah was the collector-editor of Proverbs 30 and maybe Psalms 42–89. Ruling from 715–687, Hezekiah was contemporary with the prophets Micah and Hosea, but was best acquainted with Isaiah. Hezekiah was a spiritual reformer, abolishing idolatry and reestablishing God's worship and service as was prescribed by Moses.

As a military warrior, Hezekiah openly relied on God's wisdom and power. The king was also a civil engineer, designing an ingenious water supply system for his capital city of Jerusalem.

Nahum—Jonah's Follow-up

Nineveh's revival under Jonah's ministry was only temporary. In the next century the Assyrians had reverted to their
oppression and cruelty, and Nahum announced their soon
overthrow, accurately predicting how the seemingly im-
pregnable capital, fortified by moats, walls, and high towers,
would be overcome by a combination of fire and flood.
Assyria, God's judgment tool for Israel, is now about to be
judged by Babylon.

In 612 the flooding Tigris River caused part of Nineveh's
wall to collapse, allowing the Babylonian army to enter and
burn the city. Nahum also predicted Nineveh would be hidden (3:11). So completely was Nineveh obliterated that its
remains were not discovered until A.D. 1842!

Perhaps the meaning of Nahum's name ("comfort") ap-
plies to Judah, which would be prolonged through Assyria's
demise by Babylon. Nahum's ministry from 661–612 to Nineveh, Assyria during their last four kings makes him a contemporary of the Judean prophets Zephaniah, Jeremiah, and
Habakkuk. A native of southwest Judah, Nahum lived to see
the extreme evil of Jewish kings Manasseh and Amon be
largely overcome by Josiah's spiritual revival.

Zephaniah—The Encourager

The great great grandson of godly Judean King Hezekiah,
Zephaniah ministered in Judah between 630 and 625 during
the rule of godly King Josiah. This makes him contempora-
neous with the prophets Nahum and Jeremiah. Zephaniah is
the only prophet of royal descent and lived in Jerusalem
(calling it "this place," Zeph. 1:1, 4).

The prophet's name ("Jehovah hides") may be a reference
to his and Josiah's protection during Manasseh's persecutions.

Imagine how encouraging these words of the prophet
would be to believing Hebrews close to the Babylonian Exile of Judah:

The Lord your God is with you, He is mighty to save.
He will take great delight in you, He will quiet you

with his love, He will rejoice over you with singing. ... "At that time I will gather you; at that time I will bring you home. I will give you honor and praise among all the peoples of the earth when I restore your fortunes before your very eyes," says the Lord (Zeph. 3:17, 20).

Jeremiah—The Weeping Prophet

Contemporary with the prophets Nahum, Zephaniah, Habakkuk, Daniel, and Ezekiel during the last five kings of Judah (between 627–580), Jeremiah has been dubbed the "weeping prophet" for his mourning over the sins of his people. He also suffered greatly for his faithfulness to God. Jeremiah was beaten and imprisoned for proclaiming Judah's forthcoming 70-year Babylonian Exile and urging cooperation with the conquerors. He was forbidden to marry as an object lesson to Judah that judgment was near, sparing a woman from sharing his grief.

After King Jehoiakim brazenly destroyed Jeremiah's scroll, the prophet dictated a revised version to his secretary, Baruch, who may have added the postscript about Judean King Jehoiachin's lengthened life and kind treatment in Babylon (52:31-34).

A priest living just two miles north of Jerusalem, Jeremiah's eyewitness account of that city's destruction by the Babylonians in 586 is recorded in his Book of Lamentations. This is the only Old Testament prophetic book that does not derive its name from its human author and was originally appended to the Book of Jeremiah. Lamentations is laid out as an elaborate acrostic with verses beginning with letters of the Hebrew alphabet in successive order. This is the main Scripture read and recited by orthodox Jewry today at the Jerusalem Wailing Wall, below the old temple mount.

After the Babylonian conquest, Jeremiah encouraged the Hebrew captives to accept the fact they would not come back until the predicted 70 years were fulfilled. Jeremiah's name ("Jehovah establishes") is symbolic of what God would do for His Hebrew nation.

The Talmud specifies Jeremiah as the final author-editor of the Book of Kings (originally 1 and 2 Kings were one book). This covers about 400 years of Hebrew history (from Solomon's crowning in 970 to the Babylonian Exile in 586) and was written as a continuous narrative by a succession of prophets, including Nathan, Ahijah, Iddo, Shemaiah, Jehu, and Isaiah (2 Chron. 9:29; 12:15; 13:22; 20:34; 26:22; 32:32). The last chapter of 2 Kings is anonymous.

Habakkuk—The Questioner

As a contemporary with the Prophet Jeremiah during godless King Jehoiakim's wicked years in Judah, Habakkuk questioned God's seeming inactivity about the Hebrews' iniquity. God answered that the Babylonians would judge the Jews, but the invaders would be judged for their own sins in due time. Ministering between 610–599 in Judah, Habakkuk ("one who embraces") probably witnessed Babylonian King Nebuchadnezzar's first conquest of Jerusalem in 606 and subsequent deportation of about 10,000 Jews to Babylon. Among the first group of Hebrew captives was the prophet Daniel. The musical notation appended to his book may indicate Habakkuk was a priest associated with temple worship.

Daniel—Writer in Exile

Three prophetic books were written during Judah's 70-year exile in Babylon: Daniel, Ezekiel, and Lamentations. The former two lived and wrote in Babylon, while Jeremiah penned his Lamentations in Judah.

Daniel was a contemporary with Jeremiah and Ezekiel during the last six rulers of Babylon, beginning with Nebuchadnezzar, who conquered Judah in 606 and destroyed Jerusalem in 586. At age 16 Daniel was taken with the first group of Hebrew captives to Babylon in 606.

A Babylonian official described Daniel as among "the Israelites from the royal family and the nobility—young men without any physical defect, handsome, showing aptitude for every kind of learning, well informed, quick to understand, and qualified to serve in the king's palace" (Dan. 1:3-4).

After three years of training, Daniel served in the Babylonian court for about 70 years (606–534), spanning the entire Jewish exile.

Throughout his life, Daniel remained full of faith toward God and courageous toward danger. He could not be made to compromise his deep-rooted spiritual convictions, proving the aptness of his name's meaning—"God is my judge." Daniel is famed for his God-given wisdom and ability to reveal and interpret dreams. God tells Daniel three times that he is "highly esteemed" (Dan. 9:23). His contemporary, Ezekiel, three times upholds Daniel as the highest example of a righteous person (Ezek. 14:14, 20; 28:3). Nothing negative is recorded about Daniel in Scripture.

Through Daniel God revealed His program for the Gentiles to the princely powers of Babylon. Unbelieving critics castigate Daniel for his too-specific prophecies about four world powers—Babylon, Medo-Persia, Greece, and Rome—and Cyrus, a Persian king. In his chapter 11 alone, Daniel predicts over 100 specific events, all of which have come literally true. Those with a bias against God's ability to accurately reveal the future think Daniel must have been written about 150 by a historian, not a prophet. Such a view would make Daniel deceptive in claiming to be predicting the events he describes.

A few chapters of Daniel were written in Aramaic, another Semitic language, using the same characters as Hebrew (Dan. 2:4b–7:28).

Ezekiel—The Visual Educator

While Daniel ministered in the Gentile Babylonian palace, Ezekiel was carried captive from Jerusalem to Babylon in 597 to minister to the Hebrew exiles. Jeremiah continued to minister in Judah and Egypt during this time. Jewish rebellion caused Nebuchadnezzar to attack Jerusalem a second time and take 10,000 Hebrews captive, Ezekiel and King Jehoiachin among them.

Ezekiel, whose name means "strengthened by God," was given divine power to persevere in the face of repeated rejection. His wife died as a sign of the suffering God's people would experience when the Babylonians would destroy Jerusalem in 586.

Though called by God to serve as a prophet, Ezekiel always kept his priestly interest in the temple and the sacrificial system. Though a captive, Ezekiel was allowed to preach and prophesy in Babylon. His ministry spanned over two decades from 593 to at least 571. He was the most dramatic of the prophets, often acting out his message symbolically.

Similar to Isaiah and Jeremiah, Ezekiel first wrote of Judah's suffering for her sins, and then the salvation that would follow. Ezekiel devoted half of his book to trying to convince the Jews to settle down in Babylon—a most unpopular doctrine. After news came of Jerusalem's destruction, Ezekiel's ministry turned to instilling hope in the Hebrews. He assured them they would return to their homeland and rebuild the temple.

Haggai—The Temple Prodder

The remaining Old Testament books were produced in the 100-year period of Judah's restoration from her Babylonian Exile, between 536 and 424.

Freed by Persian King Cyrus when he conquered Babylon, Zerubbabel led the first return of Jews back to Jerusalem. They laid the foundation and began to rebuild the temple in 536, but Samaritan opposition caused the work to cease for about 14 years. During this hiatus, God called Haggai and Zechariah, both returned exiles themselves, to encourage the Jews to finish the temple project.

In 520 Haggai preached four successful sermons which prodded the returnees to put a priority on God's house over further embellishing their own. Like Daniel, Haggai was born in Judah, taken captive, and lived through the 70-year exile (Hag. 2:3). Hence, Haggai could remember Jerusalem and the temple before its destruction in 586. Haggai means "festival," symbolic of the rejoicing at the temple's completion and the greater future joy when the Messiah would come to this rebuilt temple (Hag. 2:9).

Zechariah—The Messianic Anticipator

Like Ezekiel and Jeremiah and several others, Zechariah was a priest whom God also called to a prophetic ministry. Not as forceful and blunt as his older contemporary prophet Haggai (both began to preach in 520), Zechariah tried to excite the Jews about their promised Messiah. They needed to rebuild the temple because the Christ would come to it. This restoration temple, though smaller than its predecessor, would have greater glory since the Saviour would enter it.

Though greatly enlarged and embellished by King Herod the Great, Zerubbabel's temple is the one Jesus would come to in the New Testament. Zechariah gives many specific prophecies about both the first and second comings of Christ. Zechariah means "Jehovah remembers," fittingly symbolic of his emphasis on God's faithfulness to His promises to His people.

Zechariah's ministry lasted at least two years. Jewish tradition makes him a member of the Great Synagogue of Jews that collected and codified the Old Testament Scriptures. Jesus stated that Zechariah was martyred in the temple courtyard (Matt. 23:35).

Mordecai—The Influential Queen's Cousin

Mordecai is the most probable author of the Book of Esther. As Esther's cousin and a Persian court official, Mordecai was an eyewitness to the book's events and made written records (Es. 9:20). Though Jewish, both Mordecai (a descendant of Kish, the Benjamite father of King Saul) and Esther were providentially exalted in the Persian government to spare the Hebrew race from an annihilation decree.

Events in the book span about 10 years, starting with the Jewess Esther's selection as Queen of Persia in 483. Hence, Esther's story is sandwiched in the 60-year gap between chapters 6 and 7 of the Book of Ezra.

Ezra—The Major Compiler

The Talmud states Ezra wrote the book bearing his name; he writes as a first-person eyewitness (7:28ff). The book records two returns of the Jews from Babylon: one led by Zerubbabel in 536 and another led by Ezra himself in 458. The book was undoubtedly finished by the time of Nehemiah's expedition to Judah in 444. Like Daniel, a few chapters of Ezra were written in Aramaic (4:8–6:18; 7:12-26). Otherwise, all of the Old Testament was written in the language of one nation, the Hebrews.

Ezra was a priest, directly descended from the first high priest Aaron. As a "professional" Bible teacher, Ezra committed himself to understanding God's words and applying their truths to his own life before teaching them to others. "Ezra had devoted himself to the study and observance of the Law of the Lord, and to teaching its decrees and laws in Israel" (Ezra 7:10).

Ezra was well known even in secular circles. We read in Scripture, "This is a copy of the letter King Artaxerxes had given to Ezra the priest and teacher, a man learned in matters concerning the commands and decrees of the Lord for Israel: Artaxerxes, king of kings, to Ezra the priest, a teacher of the Law of the God of heaven: Greetings" (Ezra 7:11-12).

Ezra also served as a scribe, copying and preserving the Scriptures. His name means "Jehovah helps."

Ezra is also credited with completing the Chronicles (originally one book). His access to Nehemiah's extensive library would have been of great help in writing Ezra 1–6 and Chronicles (2 Maccabees 2:13-15).

First Chronicles is God's commentary on David's life, with emphasis on his family tree and preparations to build God a temple. Second Chronicles summarizes the Southern Kingdom, from Solomon to the Babylonian Exile, with each king rated according to David's heart for God.

Since Ezra and Nehemiah were originally one book, either Ezra wrote them both or Nehemiah appended his writing to Ezra's. Continuing another's history was a common practice, as Joshua, Samuel, and others had done previously. The Latin

Bible later divided the Books of Ezra and Nehemiah, calling them First and Second Ezra, respectively. Later the Book of Nehemiah was renamed for its main character. If Ezra did write Nehemiah's account, he undoubtedly used the governor's personal diary of first-person accounts.

Ezra may have compiled books 4 (90–106) and 5 (107–150) of the Psalms around 430. The remaining Old Testament Scriptures were completed within Ezra's lifetime, and tradition claims Ezra collected the biblical books. Orthodox Jews believe Ezra was the founder of the Great Synagogue, which settled the composition of the Old Testament collection. Ezra is also credited with beginning synagogues for Jewish worship during the Exile, a practice which continues down to modern times.

It's interesting that during the period of time covered by the Book of Ezra, three other religious philosophers were writing—Gautama Buddha in India, Confucius in China, and Socrates in Greece—none of whom claimed their writings were inspired by God.

Nehemiah—The Motivational Governor
In 444 God led Nehemiah ("Jehovah comforts") from Babylon to Judah to rebuild Jerusalem's walls and serve at least two terms as governor of the city. As cupbearer to the Persian King Artaxerxes, Nehemiah held a position of high trust, responsible to taste the king's food and drink to protect him from possible poisoning. Artaxerxes' stepmother was Queen Esther, the Jewess. Nehemiah is consistently depicted as a man of faith and prayer, consumed with compassion for the oppressed. He was willing to make great sacrifices to help his fellow Jews.

When Nehemiah came to Jerusalem, 92 years had passed since Zerubbabel led the first expedition home from Babylon. But the walls and gates of the Jewish capital were still in ruins. What others hadn't accomplished in nearly a century, Nehemiah motivated and organized the Jews to accomplish in a record 52 days (Neh. 6:15)!

It is uncertain if Nehemiah composed the whole book

bearing his name, or just the first-person accounts (1:1–7:5; 11:27–12:43; 13:4-31). Ezra, still serving as priest and Bible teacher, led an extended revival meeting at the Water Gate square in Jerusalem (Neh. 8:1-8).

Malachi—Last but Not Least

Malachi ministered during the latter half of Nehemiah's governorship, which may have lasted until about 414. Malachi's message best fits the Jerusalem Jews' spiritual condition during the time of Nehemiah's absence in Persia (432–425).

Nothing is known of Malachi outside of his book except a tradition claiming him to be a member of Ezra's Great Synagogue. Contemporary with Nehemiah and Ezra, Malachi ministered between 435 and 424 in Judah. Not only were the Jews entrenched in sinful ways, but they had adopted a cynical spirit—proving that Ezra's great revival was short-lived. Malachi's name means "messenger of Jehovah," and he was conscious of receiving and speaking a message from God. "An oracle: The word of the Lord to Israel through Malachi" (Mal. 1:1).

After Malachi, God's next spokesman in the world would be the angel Gabriel over 400 years later, followed by John the Baptist and Jesus.

How sad that after more than 2,000 years of revelation, redemption, and revival since Abraham's day, God's people were sinning and cynical, fending off God with self-righteous questions. A similar spirit would still be present when Messiah came in the New Testament.

The Old Testament begins with God's Creation and blessing all He had made as "good," but closes with a curse: "See, I will send you the prophet Elijah before that great and dreadful day of the Lord comes. He will turn the hearts of the fathers to their children, and the hearts of the children to their fathers; or else I will come and strike the land with a curse" (Mal. 4:5-6).

Contrast the much higher note on which the New Testament (and thus the Bible) ends. "He who testifies to these things says, 'Yes, I am coming soon.' Amen. Come, Lord

Jesus. The grace of the Lord Jesus be with God's people" (Rev. 22:20-21).

In Summary
Though the prophets knew they were recording God's words, they didn't always understand them. Even the angels in heaven are anxious to learn more about what the ancient prophets wrote:

> Concerning this salvation, the prophets, who spoke of the grace that was to come to you, searched intently and with the greatest care, trying to find out the time and circumstances to which the Spirit of Christ in them was pointing when he predicted the sufferings of Christ and the glories that would follow. It was revealed to them that they were not serving themselves but you, when they spoke of the things that have now been told you by those who have preached the Gospel to you by the Holy Spirit sent from heaven. Even angels long to look into these things (1 Peter 1:10-12).

More than 3,800 times the Old Testament writers ascribed their words to God, using phrases such as, "The Lord says..." or "Hear the word of the Lord..." (Isa. 3:16; 1:10).

All of the Old Testament authors of whom much is known were recognized prophets of God, commissioned by Him to proclaim His words by their lips and pens.

The Old Testament books were written by men from many walks of life, through whom God breathed His word. Each worked without knowledge of or collaboration with the others for the most part, yet the final product has a consistent message of salvation.

6

An Old Collection

Collecting the Old Testament Books

Many Christians wonder how the Bible got put together. Believing God was the ultimate Author, they know the completed Bible wasn't dropped from heaven or discovered in a cave. So who decided which books would be included? Are we sure the Bible contains only those books God intended? Why were some other ancient books excluded from the collection?

No one can point to a specific place and day when the completed Bible was "born." It didn't come into being like a modern book, which is written and edited, then published in finished form on a certain date.

The Bible is a collection of 66 books which grew over a 1,600-year period with the Prophet Moses as the first author and the Apostle John the last. *Bible* derives from a Greek word meaning "the books," but unlike an ordinary anthology, it was not a committee project in which scholars debated and voted on a roster of candidate books. Each Bible portion was treasured in its own right first after it was written and added to the gradually growing collection of sacred books.

The final collection of sacred books is called the *canon* of Scripture, from a Greek word meaning "a measuring stick," referring to those books which were measured by a standard and accepted as divine. The high standards for a writing to be accepted as part of the Old Testament included affirmative answers to the following questions:

● Is it divinely inspired?
● Was it written by a recognized prophet of God?
● Does it record actual facts? (i.e., is it authentic?)
● Can it be traced to the time and place of the writer? (i.e., is it genuine?)
● Has it been accepted as divinely inspired by the people of God?

The writings of Moses, Joshua, Samuel, and the other prophets were stored in the tabernacle and venerated. We have already seen how later writings were often appended to earlier ones.

Making the Collection

Only writings from God's recognized prophets were collected, as the New Testament assures us.

In the past God spoke to our forefathers through the prophets at many times and in various ways, but in these last days He has spoken to us by His Son (Heb. 1:1).

We have the word of the prophets made more certain. . . . Above all, you must understand that no prophecy of Scripture came about by the prophet's own interpretation. For prophecy never had its origin in the will of man, but men spoke from God as they were carried along by the Holy Spirit (2 Peter 1:19-21).

Individual Bible authors didn't know how their work would fit into the book's overall plan. Today, after the fact, it's easier to see how each piece of the Bible puzzle fits together perfectly.

God repeatedly exhorted the Hebrews to heed the prophets as His spokesmen, accrediting their messages with supernatural signs and fulfilled prophecies. True prophets were allowed no margin for error; if they were not 100 percent accurate, they were to be killed. Disobeying a prophet of God brought severe penalties (Deut. 13:1-5; 18:17-22).

All of the Old Testament authors of whom much is known were recognized prophets of God, commissioned by Him to proclaim His words by their lips and pens.

Not everyone who claimed to be God's spokesman was accepted as such:

> But there were also false prophets among the people, just as there will be false teachers among you. They will secretly introduce destructive heresies, even denying the sovereign Lord who bought them—bringing swift destruction on themselves. Many will follow their shameful ways and will bring the way of truth into disrepute. In their greed these teachers will exploit you with stories they have made up. Their condemnation has long been hanging over them, and their destruction has not been sleeping (2 Peter 2:1-3).

The Old Testament *Scriptures* ("sacred writings") formed an assembled collection when the last books were written in Ezra's time (about 425 B.C.). Jewish tradition says Ezra collected the remaining Old Testament books after the Jews returned from the Babylonian Exile. The invaders had destroyed or scattered many copies about 70 years earlier.

Ezra formed a council of 120 devout Jewish men, called the Great Synagogue, to restore the Hebrews' worship system. Tradition says these spiritual leaders made the final collection of the Old Testament canon.

Copy Men
For several centuries before Christ, the Jews reverenced the same Hebrew Old Testament they have today; it was the basis for their law and worship. There was no question

among the Jews about the authenticity of the collection.

For over 3,000 years—from Moses to the printing press—all copies of the Old Testament were made by hand. Scribes had to adhere to strict rules, especially in copying scrolls to be used for worship and study in Jewish synagogues:

☐ A synagogue roll must be written on the skins of clean animals, and ☐ prepared for the particular use of the synagogue by a Jew. ☐ These must be fastened together with strings taken from clean animals. ☐ Every skin must contain a certain number of columns, equal throughout the entire codex. ☐ The length of each column must not extend over less than 48 or more than 60 lines; and the breadth must consist of 30 letters. ☐ The whole copy must be first-lined; and if three words should be written without a line, it is worthless. ☐ The ink should be black, neither red, green, nor any other color, and be prepared according to a definite recipe. ☐ An authentic copy must be the exemplar, from which the transcriber ought not in the least deviate. ☐ No word or letter, not even a *yod*, must be written from memory, the scribe not having looked at the codex before him. . . . ☐ Between every consonant the space of a hair or thread must intervene; ☐ between every new *parashah*, or section, the breadth of nine consonants; ☐ between every book, three lines. ☐ The fifth book of Moses must terminate exactly with a line; but the rest need not do so. ☐ Besides this, the copyist must sit in full Jewish dress, ☐ wash his whole body, ☐ not begin to write the name of God with a pen newly dipped in ink, ☐ and should a king address him while writing that name he must take no notice of him. (Samuel Davidson, *The Hebrew Text of the Old Testament,* p. 89)

"Common copies" for private use were also made with great care but could be ornamented or include marginal notes. The Talmud specified that any biblical manuscript (handwritten copy) that contained a mistake or was worn out from use must be ceremonially buried.

When 24 Equals 39
The Hebrew Bible has fewer books, but the exact same content as modern English versions of the Old Testament. The Hebrew's number of books is reduced to 24 from 39 by combining the pairs of Samuels, Kings, Chronicles, and Ezra–Nehemiah into one book each. They also group the 12 Minor Prophets into one book, *The Twelve*.

Our English arrangement stems from the *Septuagint*, the Greek version of the Old Testament discussed below. Note the Hebrew and English Old Testament books listed in Chart 4. (For easier comparison, the second column is changed from the Hebrew order).

OLD TESTAMENT BOOKS IN ENGLISH AND HEBREW
(Chart 4)

ENGLISH BIBLE	HEBREW BIBLE
1 Genesis	1 Genesis
2 Exodus	2 Exodus
3 Leviticus	3 Leviticus
4 Numbers	4 Numbers
5 Deuteronomy	5 Deuteronomy
6 Joshua	6 Joshua
7 Judges	7 Judges
8 Ruth	8 Ruth
9 1 Samuel	9 Samuel (combines both Samuels as one)
10 2 Samuel	
11 1 Kings	10 Kings (combines both Kings as one)
12 2 Kings	
13 1 Chronicles	11 Chronicles (combines both Chronicles as one)
14 2 Chronicles	

15 Ezra	12 Ezra-Nehemiah (combines Ezra and Nehemiah as one)
16 Nehemiah	
17 Esther	13 Esther
18 Job	14 Job
19 Psalms	15 Psalms
20 Proverbs	16 Proverbs
21 Ecclesiastes	17 Ecclesiastes
22 Song of Solomon	18 Song of Solomon
23 Isaiah	19 Isaiah
24 Jeremiah	20 Jeremiah
25 Lamentations	21 Lamentations
26 Ezekiel	22 Ezekiel
27 Daniel	23 Daniel
28 Hosea	24 Book of the Twelve (combines Hosea–Malachi as one)
29 Joel	(Included in Book of the Twelve)
30 Amos	(Included in Book of the Twelve)
31 Obadiah	(Included in Book of the Twelve)
32 Jonah	(Included in Book of the Twelve)
33 Micah	(Included in Book of the Twelve)
34 Nahum	(Included in Book of the Twelve)
35 Habakkuk	(Included in Book of the Twelve)
36 Zephaniah	(Included in Book of the Twelve)
37 Haggai	(Included in Book of the Twelve)
38 Zechariah	(Included in Book of the Twelve)
39 Malachi	(Included in Book of the Twelve)
39 books in English OT =	24 books in Hebrew OT

Much evidence exists as to which books were considered part of the Hebrews' sacred collection.

It's Greek to Me

The *Septuagint*, a translation of the Hebrew Old Testament into Greek about 250 B.C., bears silent witness that the Old Testament canon was complete before that time. Only those books considered divine were translated. In addition to the Dead Sea Scrolls of the Essenes, probably the most significant writing of the intertestamental times was the Septuagint. Made in Alexandria, Egypt, it derived its name from the supposedly 72 translators who worked on the project (6 from each of the 12 Jewish tribes). Since Hebrew was becoming a dead language, the Septuagint (often called the LXX, Roman numeral for 70) made the Scriptures available in the main language of that day.

Comparing the Septuagint with the standard Hebrew Old Testament text from 1,100 years later (about A.D. 900) shows extremely close correlation between these two independent documents, adding to our confidence in the reliable preservation of the Scriptures.

The 22 books of the Hebrew Bible were subdivided into 39 books at the time of this version (Chart 4). The Hebrews organized their Scriptures into three categories:

1. Law (Genesis–Deuteronomy)
2. Prophets (Joshua–Kings; Isaiah, Jeremiah, Ezekiel, The Twelve)
3. Writings (all the rest).

The Greek-speaking Jews reorganized the Old Testament into three different categories:

1. Law and History (Genesis–Deuteronomy)
2. Poetry (Job–Song of Solomon)
3. Prophecy (Isaiah–Malachi)

See Chart 5 for the Hebrew arrangement of the Old Testament and Chart 6 for the Greek Old Testament arrangement. Bibles in English follow the Greek groupings.

Modern Hebrew Bibles have 24 books instead of 22 by separating Lamentations from Jeremiah and Ruth from Judges.

HEBREW OLD TESTAMENT ARRANGEMENT
(Chart 5)

LAW (TORAH)	PROPHETS	WRITINGS
1 Genesis	Former Prophets	Poetical Books
2 Exodus	6 Joshua	14 Psalms
3 Leviticus	7 Judges	15 Proverbs
4 Numbers	8 Samuel	16 Job
5 Deuteronomy	9 Kings	Five Rolls
	Latter Prophets	17 Song of Solomon
	10 Isaiah	18 Ruth
	11 Jeremiah	19 Lamentations
	12 Ezekiel	20 Esther
	13 The Twelve	21 Ecclesiastes
		Historical Books
		22 Daniel
		23 Ezra–Nehemiah
		24 Chronicles

GREEK AND ENGLISH OLD TESTAMENT ARRANGEMENT
(Chart 6)

LAW AND HISTORY	POETRY	PROPHECY
Law (Pentateuch)	18 Job	Major Prophets
1 Genesis	19 Psalms	23 Isaiah
2 Exodus	20 Proverbs	24 Jeremiah
3 Leviticus	21 Ecclesiastes	25 Lamentations
4 Numbers	22 Song of Solomon	26 Ezekiel
5 Deuteronomy		27 Daniel
History		Minor Prophets
6 Joshua		28 Hosea
7 Judges		29 Joel

8 Ruth	30 Amos
9 1 Samuel	31 Obadiah
10 2 Samuel	32 Jonah
11 1 Kings	33 Micah
12 2 Kings	34 Nahum
13 1 Chronicles	35 Habakkuk
14 2 Chronicles	36 Zephaniah
15 Ezra	37 Haggai
16 Nehemiah	38 Zechariah
17 Esther	39 Malachi

One of the most famous ancient Bible manuscripts in existence today, Codex Alexandrinus, dates from about A.D. 450 and is named for its place of origin, Alexandria, Egypt. "Codex A" contains the Septuagint plus the New Testament in Greek, and is on public display at the British Museum in London.

Scrolls from the Dead Sea

The now-famous scrolls discovered between 1947 and 1956 in the Qumran caves on the western shores of the Dead Sea in Israel date from about 200 B.C. Extremists in isolation, the Jewish monastic Essenes, producers of the scrolls, tried to escape the corruption of civil and religious life by retreating to desert caves. Handwritten copies of every Old Testament book except Esther have been found so far. These Hebrew Old Testament manuscripts are about 1,100 years older than any previously found.

Before 1947, there were four known manuscripts of the Old Testament in Hebrew, produced about A.D. 900. Now there are thousands of fragments and copies of whole books dating from at least a century before Christ. Seeing the similarity of these 1,100-year-apart copies provides overwhelming confirmation of the accuracy of copies of the biblical documents. Two Qumran copies of Isaiah made about 200 B.C. are over 95-percent word-for-word identical to the standard Hebrew text from over a thousand years later. The 5-

percent variation consists mainly of obvious scribal errors and spelling variations.

In Isaiah 53, for example, only 17 letters vary among the 166 words in this chapter. Ten letters are spelling differences, 4 are conjunction changes, and the remaining 3 letters form the word for "light" in verse 11. The latter is the only substantive change and doesn't greatly affect the meaning.

Is it possible God allowed minor variations in copies of the Bible texts so people wouldn't worship any one copy as the "original"? Nonetheless, the reliability of the Bible's manuscripts is greater than that of any other documents which have come down to us from antiquity.

Other literature of the Essenes quotes from the Torah (Genesis–Deuteronomy), Psalms, Proverbs, and many prophets as authoritative. It will take scholars at least another decade to piece together remaining unclassified fragments in the Dead Sea Scrolls collection.

Jesus on the Old Testament

The Lord Jesus Christ confirmed the authority of the Old Testament, calling it the Word of God and assuring His followers that every word of it would be fulfilled.

Jesus said:

> I tell you the truth, until heaven and earth disappear, not the smallest letter, not the least stroke of a pen, will by any means disappear from the Law until everything is accomplished. Anyone who breaks one of the least of these commandments and teaches others to do the same will be called least in the kingdom of heaven, but whoever practices and teaches these commands will be called great in the kingdom of heaven (Matt. 5:18-19).

Speaking to the Jewish religious leaders of His day, Jesus challenged their exaltation of tradition over the Old Testament, calling the latter the "command of God" and the "word of God" (Matt. 15:3-6). One tenth of Jesus' recorded spoken words were taken from the Old Testament.

Jesus ordered His earthly life by the Old Testament Scriptures, taught and interpreted their principles, and appealed to them as the ultimate authority in temptation or dispute. Jesus said Moses and his writings were a more powerful witness from God than someone rising from the dead and testifying about the afterlife (Luke 16:31)! Our Lord's view of the Old Testament settles the issue for most Christians; the authority of Christ and Scripture stand together.

Jesus' apostles shared their Master's view of the Old Testament. Peter said of it, "Prophecy never had its origin in the will of man, but men spoke from God as they were carried along by the Holy Spirit" (2 Peter 1:21). Paul declared, "All Scripture is God-breathed and is useful for teaching, rebuking, correcting and training in righteousness" (2 Tim. 3:16).

The 278 quotations of and 613 allusions to the Old Testament as the "holy Scriptures," "word of God," and other terms of veneration in the New Testament show Christ and His apostles accepted the Hebrew canon of Scripture. Ten percent of the New Testament text is quotation from the Old Testament as authoritative Scripture!

Do We Have Jesus' Old Testament?

Our Old Testament books are unquestionably the ones received and believed by Jesus and His apostles as the Scriptures. The New Testament quotes from nearly all 39 books as authoritative. Of the New Testament's 260 chapters, 209 quote the Old Testament. The New Testament is unanimous in considering the former Testament a completed unit with a continuous story, calling it all "the Law" or "the Law and the Prophets."

In describing all the martyred prophets from Creation to the conclusion of the Old Testament, Jesus said to the Jewish leaders of His day:

This generation will be held responsible for the blood of all the prophets that has been shed since the beginning of the world, from the blood of Abel to the blood of Zechariah, who was killed between the altar and the sanctuary (Luke 11:50-51).

Jesus said the Old Testament revelation spanned from Genesis, the first book in the Hebrew Bible, which records Abel's murder, to 2 Chronicles, the last book in the Hebrew Bible, which records Zechariah's martyrdom. This is the exact equivalent of our referring to the whole Old Testament in English as "from Genesis to Malachi."

Josephus, a respected Jewish historian and contemporary of the New Testament apostles (A.D. 37–95), said no Hebrew Scriptures were added after the time of the Persian King Artaxerxes (464–424 B.C.), the era of Ezra, Nehemiah, and Malachi. Josephus' reason is:

> Because the exact succession of the prophets ceased ...no one has dared to add anything to them, or to take anything from them, or to alter anything in them... only 22 books, which contain the records of all time, and are justly believed to be divine (*Against Apion*, 1:8).

Josephus combined Ruth with Judges and Lamentations with Jeremiah to make 22 books from the Hebrews' 24. Leaving no room for doubt, Josephus named the 22 books in the Hebrew Old Testament.

Council Considerations

About A.D. 90 at Jamnia (or Jabneh, a town near Joppa, Israel), an official council of Jewish leaders ratified the Old Testament canon, which had already been accepted for nearly 500 years. During their deliberations, they raised some new questions about five Old Testament books. But closer scrutiny resolved their questions.

The council debated why Esther did not mention God's name, the only Hebrew Scripture book to omit it. They decided God's presence, power, and protection was evident

in the Book of Esther in His saving the Jewish race from a
Persian king's annihilation decree.

It's interesting that in an ancient Hebrew manuscript of
Esther, God's name *is* found four times as an acrostic, reading single letters vertically. It occurs twice in the first column of letters along the left margin and twice in the last
column on the right. Two of the mentions read down and
two read up. Is it possible some Hebrew scribe tried to
amend for the seeming omission?

Proverbs was questioned as perhaps being self-contradic-
tory. For example, "Do not answer a fool according to his
folly, or you will be like him yourself. Answer a fool according to his folly, or he will be wise in his own eyes" (Prov.
26:4-5). But these apparently contradictory Proverbs apply
to different situations because a different Hebrew word is
used for "fool" in each verse. Some types of fools will receive correction; others won't.

Ecclesiastes seemed skeptical to the Jamnia council, pre-
senting a humanistic view of life out of keeping with the
tenor of Scripture. But they concluded God was not
condoning what Ecclesiastes recorded, and that the book
presents an accurate description of humanity's search for
meaning in life apart from God. Elsewhere Scripture records
statements by the devil or evil men, giving an accurate
record of what they said without condoning it.

Solomon concludes, "Remember your Creator in the days
of your youth, before the days of trouble come and the
years approach when you will say, 'I find no pleasure in
them' " (Ecc. 12:1).

The Song of Solomon was challenged for seeming to emphasize the sensual side of marriage, which was not in keeping with Jewish culture. Orthodox Jews forbade their young
men to read the Song until they were at least 30 years of
age! But God created humanity male and female and established the sexual union in marriage. The Jamnia Jews accepted the Song of Solomon as a picture of God's love for
Israel.

Ezekiel's description of the Jewish temple in chapters

40–48 differs from Moses' in Exodus 25–40. But Ezekiel's temple is prophetic of a permanent one to be built when Messiah comes. Moses describes a portable tabernacle.

Such questioning helps assure us that succeeding generations didn't unthinkingly accept what they received. No Old Testament book was removed from the sacred collection, and other ancient books were flatly rejected at Jamnia.

Why Do Catholics Have a Bigger Bible?

For about 1,900 years after their completion, only the 39 Old Testament books as we know them were considered sacred. It was not until A.D. 1546 that part of Christendom accepted additional books into the canon.

Many books known as *apocrypha* ("hidden") were produced between 200 B.C. and A.D. 100. These apocryphal books were not accepted as Scripture by anyone until, in reaction to the Protestant Reformers, the Council of Trent added some of them to the Roman Catholic Bible in 1546. Challenged by the new Protestants to show Scriptural support for such practices as praying for the dead and receiving forgiveness for sins by doing good deeds, the Catholic Church council found justification in the apocryphal literature and added it to their Old Testament.

Because some pieces of apocryphal literature were appended to existing Scriptural books, the Roman Catholic Old Testament has 46 separate books compared to the Protestants' 39. The extras are summarized in Chart 7.

The New Testament never quotes from the apocrypha which the Roman Catholic Church later adopted, nor were these extra books accepted by Jerome, who made the Catholics' official Latin version about 400. The Apocrypha doesn't claim to be Scripture or the work of prophets, but provides an interesting history of the times between the Bible's two Testaments.

Pseudepigraphic books make spurious claims of authorship or time of writing. Most were attempts to fill gaps in the sacred record, but no one accepted them as authoritative or authentic. Seven major pseudepigraphic works pro-

CATHOLIC ADDITIONS TO THE OLD TESTAMENT IN 1546
(Chart 7)

APOCRYPHAL BOOK:	IN ROMAN CATHOLIC BIBLE AS:
1. The Wisdom of Solomon (ca. 30 B.C.)	Book of Wisdom
2. Ecclesiasticus (Sirach) (132 B.C.)	Ecclesiastes
3. Tobit (ca. 200 B.C.)	Tobias
4. Judith (ca. 150 B.C.)	Judith
5. 1 Maccabees (ca. 100 B.C.)	1 Machabees
6. 2 Maccabees (ca. 110–70 B.C.)	2 Machabees
7. Baruch (ca. 150–50 B.C.)	Baruch 1–5
8. Letter of Jeremiah (ca. 300–100 B.C.)	Baruch 6
9. Additions to Esther (140–130 B.C.)	Esther 10:4–16:24
10. Prayer of Azariah (2nd or 1st century B.C.) (Song of Three Young Men)	Daniel 3:24-90
11. Susanna (2nd or 1st century B.C.)	Daniel 13
12. Bel and the Dragon (ca. 100 B.C.)	Daniel 14
13. Prayer of Manasseh (2nd or 1st century B.C.)	Prayer of Manasseh

duced between the Testaments are: Ascension of Isaiah, Assumption of Moses, Book of Enoch, Book of Jubilees, Psalter of Solomon, Sibylan Oracles, and Testament of 12 Patriarchs.

The Counter-Preservers
Between A.D. 400–900, a group of Jewish scribes called the Masoretes devoted themselves to the standardization and preservation of the Hebrew text of the Old Testament. They carefully copied the best manuscripts available and invented a system of vowel markings to preserve proper pronunciation.

In their great reverence for the sacred Scriptures, the Masoretes counted the number of letters and words on each page and in each Bible book, even indicating the center letters. How many letters are on this page? What is the center letter? Can you imagine counting all the letters in the Book of Genesis, then in the entire Old Testament?

The Masoretes counted everything countable regarding the Hebrew text in their efforts to make verifiably accurate copies possible before the invention of modern printing.

It's inevitable that slight variations still crept into hand-written copies of such long manuscripts over so many centuries. The 22 letters of the Hebrew alphabet and their English names and values are depicted in the chart below. Note the similarity of He, Cheth, and Taw. Gimel and Nun are also similar, as are Beth and Kaph. Also compare Mem with Teth and Waw with Zayin.

THE HEBREW ALPHABET
(CHART 8)

The Hebrew alphabet, reading right to left, has 22 basic consonants.

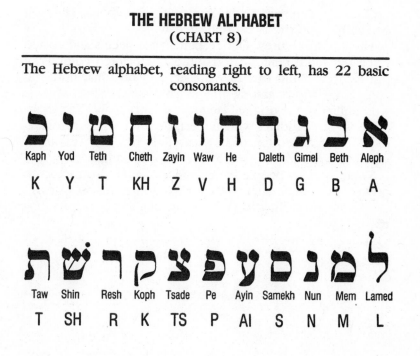

Kaph	Yod	Teth	Cheth	Zayin	Waw	He	Daleth	Gimel	Beth	Aleph
K	Y	T	KH	Z	V	H	D	G	B	A

Taw	Shin	Resh	Koph	Tsade	Pe	Ayin	Samekh	Nun	Mem	Lamed
T	SH	R	K	TS	P	AI	S	N	M	L

Imagine copying page after page of such consonants with no intervening spaces! Genesis 1:1 would appear as follows, using English letters for examples. Remember, Hebrew reads from right to left without vowels.

HTRHTDNSNVHHTDTRCDGGNNNGBHTN

Try copying the above line a few times and check your accuracy. Or, just copy this simple English sentence.

It's fun to be in
in Paris in the
the spring.

Carefully compare your copy with the above. Did you correctly copy the two duplicated words?

Though the Hebrew Old Testament has been standardized since the tenth century, today modern printed editions of the Hebrew Bible carefully preserve in marginal notes all known variations among the extant manuscripts. Anyone with ability in the original language can compare the variant options. But scholars who undertake such tasks are unanimous in their acclaim of how carefully the Old Testament text has been transmitted in the Hebrew language.

Since so many people have expended such great effort to preserve the Bible accurately for us, how much investment should we be willing to make in reading and understanding it?

7

From Brothers to Murderers

The New Testament Writers, Part 1

Many aspects distinguished the making of the New Testament from the Old.

The Old Testament had been given in the language of one nation—the Hebrews. The New Testament was written in Greek, the international trade language of the Roman Empire, making God's new revelation immediately readable by nearly everyone.

Unlike Hebrew words, which often have a pool of meanings, Greek's larger vocabulary made it much easier to teach doctrine with precise technical terms. The differences between redemption, adoption, propitiation, justification, substitution, and sanctification are more easily conveyed in Greek. Dr. Luke uses a word reserved strictly for a surgical sewing needle when he compares a person trusting in riches to a camel going through the eye of a needle (Luke 18:25), whereas the Hebrew and Aramaic only has one term for any small opening.

Archaeological finds have confirmed that the Greek used for the New Testament is the common ("koine") language of the time, setting an example for God's words to be in the vernacular when translated. Such discoveries also provide rich illustrations of how words were used outside of the Bible. "Tetelestai," for example, spoken by Jesus from the Cross, is translated, "It is finished" (John 19:30). Thousands of bills of sale have been found with "tetelestai" inscribed across them. The meaning is obviously, "paid in full," Jesus' sacrifice on the Cross is complete payment for all sins.

New Testament writing was done with pen and ink on papyrus, paper's predecessor, made by pressing and rolling together the inner soft parts of reeds. Short letters, such as 2 or 3 John or Jude, would fit on a single sheet of papyrus.

Papyrus sheets were glued together end-to-end into long strips and rolled around two sticks to form scrolls, such as had previously been done with parchment. By turning a stick in each hand, a reader could easily access any part of a longer document. At first each book was a separate sheet or scroll. Any of the longest New Testament books, such as Matthew, Luke, or Acts, would fit on a roll about 30 feet long—the longest practical length.

Since the entire New Testament on one roll would be over 200 feet in length—a physical impossibility—the earliest Bibles were a collection of scrolls in a box or bucket! This also helps to explain why early collections of the Scriptures varied.

In the second century, bound volumes of cut sheets replaced scrolls, making it easier to publish longer works. This modern book form is called a "codex."

Produced between A.D. 50 and 100, the New Testament was written in about one thirtieth the time needed to complete the Old. But, then, the New Testament is only one-fourth the size of the Old.

God used apostles instead of Hebrew prophets, including at least one Gentile (Luke). In contrast to the 41 known authors for the Old Testament, there are only 9 or 10 New Testament authors. See Chart 9 for a chronological listing of them and a summary of their writings and occupations.

The following discussion of the nine men whom God

used to author the New Testament takes them in the order in which they wrote. For a fuller discussion of the historical background or survey of each New Testament book, consult a Bible dictionary or introductory notes in a study/reference Bible.

James—Jesus' Half Brother

After Jesus' birth to the Virgin Mary, she and Joseph had other children, making them half brothers and sisters of Jesus. Among them are James and Jude (also translated Judas), authors of the New Testament books bearing their names.

Scripture mentions these men as they are pointed out by townspeople early in Jesus' public ministry:

> Coming to His hometown, He began teaching the people in their synagogue, and they were amazed. "Where did this man get this wisdom and these miraculous powers?" they asked. "Isn't this the carpenter's son? Isn't his mother's name Mary, and aren't his brothers James, Joseph, Simon and Judas? Aren't all his sisters with us? Where then did this man get all these things?" (Matt. 13:54-56)

Tradition says James and his brothers learned the carpentry trade from their father Joseph.

This James is not to be confused with two other men in the New Testament with the name, both apostles of Christ. Author James was neither an apostle nor a believer in Christ's deity until after Jesus rose from the dead. Late in His ministry, Jesus' brothers said to Him:

> "You ought to leave here and go to Judea, so that Your disciples may see the miracles You do. No one who wants to become a public figure acts in secret. Since you are doing these things, show yourself to the world." For even His own brothers did not believe in Him (John 7:3-5).

But in describing Christ's followers who were gathered in Jerusalem after He ascended to heaven, Luke says:

Those present were Peter, John, James and Andrew; Philip and Thomas, Bartholomew and Matthew; James son of Alphaeus and Simon the Zealot, and Judas son of James. They all joined together constantly in prayer, along with the women and Mary the mother of Jesus, and with His *brothers* (Acts 1:13-14; italics added).

Note that Jesus' brothers are present among the believers, and they are specifically noted as separate from the three apostles named Judas (Jude) and James.

Jesus' resurrection and subsequent appearance to His half brother James convinced him to believe in His deity. "Then He appeared to James, then to all the apostles" (1 Cor. 15:7).

After his conversion to Christ, Paul records:

Then after three years, I went up to Jerusalem to get acquainted with Peter and stayed with him fifteen days. I saw none of the other apostles—only James, the Lord's brother. . . . James, Peter and John, those reputed to be pillars, gave me and Barnabas the right hand of fellowship when they recognized the grace given to me. They agreed that we should go to the Gentiles, and they to the Jews (Gal. 1:18-19; 2:9).

James is now considered an apostle and pillar in the Jerusalem church.

After their first missionary journey, when Paul and Barnabas "came to Jerusalem, they were welcomed by the church and the apostles and elders, to whom they reported everything God had done through them. . . . When they finished, James spoke up: 'Brothers, listen to me'" (Acts 15:4, 13).

James became prominent in the Jerusalem church and chaired the first church council. His wise summary and counsel regarding the relationship of Gentiles to Jews in the church averted a split.

Later, as Paul's companion on his third missionary journey, Luke says, "When we arrived at Jerusalem, the brothers received us warmly. The next day Paul and the rest of us went to see James, and all the elders were present. Paul greeted them and reported in detail what God had done among the Gentiles through his ministry" (Acts 21:17-19). Note the prominent place of James in the church.

God used this Jew from Nazareth to record five chapters of a book bearing his name, probably the first book of the New Testament to be written, perhaps as early as A.D. 45. James wrote as "a servant of God and of the Lord Jesus Christ" (1:1). The Book of James is a strong defense of the truth that true faith in Christ will show itself in the believer's good deeds.

James wrote from experience because church father Eusebius says James was surnamed "the Just" because of his exemplary life. Other ancient traditions say James developed "camel's knees," large callouses from extended kneeling in prayer to his divine half Brother.

James, whose name means "whom God protects," lived to about the age of 70, when he suffered a violent martyr's death just before Jerusalem's destruction in 70. (All dates in this chapter are A.D. unless noted otherwise.)

Paul—Missionary to the Gentiles

Paul is introduced in the Book of Acts as Saul, a zealous Jew whose intent was "to destroy the church. Going from house to house, he dragged off men and women and put them in prison." When church deacon and preacher Stephen was being killed at Saul's direction, Stephen's dying prayer, "Lord, do not hold this sin against them," was soon answered (see Acts 7:58–8:3).

Dr. Luke describes what happened.

Meanwhile, Saul was still breathing out murderous threats against the Lord's disciples. He went to the high priest and asked him for letters to the synagogues in Damascus, so that if he found any there who belonged to the Way, whether men or women, he might take them as prisoners to Jerusalem. As he neared Damascus on his journey, suddenly a light from heaven flashed around him. He fell to the ground and heard a voice say to him, "Saul, Saul, why do you persecute me?"

"Who are you, Lord?" Saul asked.

"I am Jesus, whom you are persecuting," He replied. "Now get up and go into the city, and you will be told what you must do."

. . . .

Yet Saul grew more and more powerful and baffled the Jews living in Damascus by proving that Jesus is the Christ (Acts 9:1-6, 22).

Saul's name (meaning "asked for") was changed to Paul ("little"), perhaps as a lifelong reminder that without Christ he could do nothing.

Born in Tarsus in the Roman province of Cilicia, Paul inherited Roman citizenship and all its privileges from his father, who also was a Pharisee, the most conservative and separated Jewish subgroup (Acts 22:28; 23:6). A tentmaker by trade, Paul also studied Hebrew law and tradition in Jerusalem under the renown teacher Gamaliel (Acts 22:3). In his zeal for Judaism, he thought he was serving God by killing Christians.

After his dramatic conversion to Christ at about age 35 (tradition says he was born two years after Christ), Paul spent 12 years being trained in his new faith. In 46 he took the first of three missionary journeys to extend Christianity throughout the Roman Empire, mainly among the Gentiles (non-Jews).

In 48, back from his first journey at his home church in Antioch of Syria, Paul sent the first of 13 letters which would be preserved forever in the New Testament. Each of Paul's letters is named for the church or individual receiving it (letters *to* the Galatians and *to* Timothy, for example).

Chart 10 (page 99) summarizes when and where each New Testament book was written.

In his letter to the new Galatian Christians, Paul claimed that his message and authority were directly from God.

> Paul, an apostle—sent not from men nor by man, but by Jesus Christ and God the Father, who raised Him from the dead . . . I want you to know, brothers, that the Gospel I preached is not something that man made up. I did not receive it from any man, nor was I taught it; rather, I received it by revelation from Jesus Christ. For you have heard of my previous way of life in Judaism, how intensely I persecuted the church of God and tried to destroy it. I was advancing in Judaism beyond many Jews of my own age and was extremely zealous for the traditions of my fathers. But when God, who set me apart from birth and called me by His grace, was pleased to reveal His Son in me so that I might preach Him among the Gentiles, I did not consult any man . . . I was personally unknown to the churches of Judea that are in Christ. They only heard the report: "The man who formerly persecuted us is now preaching the faith he once tried to destroy." And they praised God because of me. . . . They saw that I had been entrusted with the task of preaching the Gospel to the Gentiles, just as Peter had been to the Jews. For God, who was at work in the ministry of Peter as an apostle to the Jews, was also at work in my ministry as an apostle to the Gentiles (Gal. 1:1, 11-16, 22-24; 2:7-8).

Paul was concerned lest his new converts be diverted from simple faith in Christ to a scheme of Jewish works. Paul wrote the Galatian letter personally, instead of using a scribe, his normal practice (6:11).

After meeting with James and the first church council in Jerusalem to defend his work among the Gentiles, Paul embarked on a second missionary venture in 50 that would last nearly three years. While in Corinth, Greece in 52, Paul wrote 1 and 2 Thessalonians, admonishing these new converts to remain faithful to Christ until death or His return for them.

On his third missionary journey, beginning in 54 and lasting almost 4 years, Paul wrote three letters: 1 Corinthians from Ephesus to solve many specific church problems; 2 Corinthians from Macedonia to defend his apostolic authority under attack; and Romans from Corinth to declare God's righteousness was available freely to all mankind, not just to forgive sin, but also to empower for righteous living. Paul dictated Romans to his secretary, Tertius, who added his personal greeting near the end (16:22).

He who had imprisoned Christians is now incarcerated for being one, first for nearly three years in Israel, then for two years in Rome. During his first Roman imprisonment about 61, Paul wrote four letters to as many churches. Like Romans, Colossians is sent to a church Paul had neither founded nor visited. Because the Lord Jesus Christ holds the place of absolute supremacy in His universe, He alone is worthy to be submitted to and served.

In Ephesians Paul informs the Christians of their privileges and responsibilities as members of Christ' body. Philemon is an appeal to a Christian in Colossae to forgive and restore his newly converted runaway slave, Onesimus. Philippians is a thank-you letter for that church's help to Paul with encouragement to be united around Christ's attitude of servanthood.

During a period of freedom in 62 when Paul revisited some of his churches, he wrote from Macedonia to two of his pastors—Timothy in Ephesus and Titus on the island of Crete. Both received practical directions for appointing and training leadership as well as how to relate to different types of people in the churches they served.

Imprisoned again in Rome in 67 and awaiting trial, Paul wrote a second letter, his last, to Timothy, his son in the faith and long-time companion, urging him to be a faithful soldier of Christ and combat false teaching. Paul himself was faithful unto death, being decapitated by a Roman sword. In the ultimate irony, he who had killed Christians is now killed for being one.

God used this forgiven persecutor-turned-preacher to write 87 chapters of the New Testament. If Paul also wrote the Book of Hebrews, he is the most prolific New Testament author; otherwise, Dr. Luke holds that record.

The following article, "Would You Want to Hire This Man for Your Church?" shows that God can use *anyone* to accomplish His work in the world.

A certain church found itself suddenly without a pastor, and a committee was formed to search for a new man. In due course, the committee received a letter from a clergyman applying for the position. The letter went like this:

"Gentlemen: Understanding that your pulpit is vacant, I should like to submit my application. I am generally considered to be a good preacher. I have been a leader in some of the places I have served. I have also found time to do some writing on the side.

"I am over 50 years of age, and while my health is not the best, I still manage to get enough work done so as to please any parish.

"As for references, I am somewhat handicapped. I have never preached in any place for more than three years. And the churches I have preached in have generally been pretty small, even though they were located in rather large cities. In some places, I had to leave because my ministry caused riots and disturbances. Even where I stayed, I did not get along too well with other religious leaders in town, which may influence the kind of references these places will send you. I have been threatened several times and even physically attacked. Three or four times I have gone to jail for witnessing to my convictions.

"Still, I feel sure I can bring vitality to your church even though I am not particularly good at keeping records. I have to admit I don't even remember all those whom I've baptized. However, if you can use me, I should be pleased to be considered."

Hearing the letter read aloud, the committee members were aghast. How could anyone think that a church like theirs could consider a man who was nothing but a troublemaking, absentminded, ex-jailbird? What was his name?

"Well," said the chairman of the committee, "the letter is simply signed Paul."

(quoted by Richard N. Bolles in "The Episcopalian," © 1966, The Episcopalian, Inc.; used by permission).

8

From Servants to Fishermen

The New Testament Writers, Part 2

As Peter's spiritual son, John Mark had a close association with the Apostle, which gave extra authority to his writing. Peter was a regular guest at Mark's large home in Jerusalem, his voice being recognized by a house servant at night (Acts 12:12-16).

A Roman citizen and servant himself, Mark wrote his Gospel for the Romans from Rome, weaving his topical account of Jesus' life around the core of service and sacrifice. "For even the Son of Man did not come to be served, but to serve, and to give his life as a ransom for many" (Mark 10:45).

Mark omits or explains Jewish customs, interprets Aramaic words, and replaces Greek words with Latin equivalents. Mark's was probably the first Gospel account, produced between 55 and 60. Many feel Mark makes reference to himself as the young man who fled naked from Gethsemane when Jesus was arrested (14:51-52).

Mark served as a helper to the Apostle Paul and his cousin Barnabas on at least two foreign missionary trips (Acts

12:25; 13:5; 15:36-37). He ministered to Paul during his first Roman imprisonment (Col. 4:10). When imprisoned again, Paul wrote to Timothy, "Only Luke is with me. Get Mark and bring him with you, because he is helpful to me in my ministry" (2 Tim. 4:11).

Early tradition says Mark was sent by Peter on an evangelistic mission to Egypt and founded the church in Alexandria, which became a major center of Christianity in the second century. Mark was martyred in Roman Emperor Nero's eighth year.

Matthew—The Tax Collector

Matthew, also called Levi, earned his living as a Jew in Capernaum collecting taxes for the Romans—an unpopular post. Such "publicans" were considered sinners on a par with harlots and assumed to be criminals and traitors. Matthew would have bid for a Roman franchise to tax his fellow Jews.

When called from his tax booth to follow Christ, Matthew readily responded, hosting a reception in his home to introduce his friends to Christ (Matt. 9:9-10). Perhaps Levi's conscience had already been pricked by Jesus' public preaching.

Jesus later appointed him as one of His first 12 Apostles, along with 4 fishermen from whom Matthew had previously extorted excess taxes! No further mention is made of Matthew except in lists of the apostles and to mention his presence with the believers in Jerusalem waiting for the Holy Spirit (Acts 1:13). Matthew means "gift of God."

Matthew later wrote his Gospel (meaning "good news") to his fellow Jews to prove that Jesus is the Messiah promised in the Old Testament. Over 120 quotations and allusions to the former Testament are marshaled as evidence that Jesus fulfills the Hebrew prophecies of the Saviour. Matthew was probably written in Jerusalem between 55 and 65, providing 28 chapters of the New Testament.

Tradition says Matthew preached in Judea for 12–15 years after Jesus' ascension before serving as a foreign missionary, dying as a martyr in Ethiopia.

Luke—The Beloved Physician

As a Greek physician, Dr. Luke is well qualified to write an account of Jesus' life emphasizing His being the perfect Man. Since Luke had not been an eyewitness of Jesus' life, he relies on careful research and accounts by those who had been with Jesus.

> Many have undertaken to draw up an account of the things that have been fulfilled among us, just as they were handed down to us by those who from the first were eyewitnesses and servants of the word. Therefore, since I myself have carefully investigated everything from the beginning, it seemed good also to me to write an orderly account for you, most excellent Theophilus, so that you may know the certainty of the things you have been taught (Luke 1:1-4).

Luke later wrote the Book of Acts as a continuation of his research project for his friend Theophilus ("lover of God"). Nowhere in his two books does Luke identify himself by name as the author, but strong tradition claims it to be Luke. Portions of Acts are first-person accounts by a close traveling companion of the Apostle Paul (16:1-17; 20:5–21:18; 27:1–28:16). Standing by Paul during both of his Roman imprisonments, Luke is called "the beloved physician" by his apostolic friend (Col. 4:14; 2 Tim. 4:11).

Probably from Antioch, Luke is the only non-Jewish New Testament author, who, interestingly, wrote the most of it (52 chapters or 2,158 verses). Luke wrote more verses in 2 books than Paul did in 13 (unless Paul also wrote Hebrews). Luke probably wrote both books from Rome between 60 and 62, having access to eyewitnesses and written records in addition to his own diary. Mixed traditions say Luke died as a martyr or of natural causes at age 84.

Peter—The Big Fisherman

Jews from Bethsaida, Peter and his brother Andrew were partners in a fishing business on the Sea of Galilee with two other apostles of Christ—James and John (Matt. 4:18; Luke 5:10). Jesus changed his name from Simon ("hearer") to Peter ("a rock") at their first meeting (John 1:36-42).

Later Peter and his three partners responded to Jesus' call to follow Him and fish for men. Peter, James, and John formed an inner circle with Jesus during His earthly ministry. They alone, for example, witnessed Jesus' transfiguration (Matt. 17).

Though sometimes exhibiting an impetuous nature, Peter was the first disciple to publicly affirm Christ's deity, saying, "You are the Christ, the Son of the living God" (Matt. 16:16). Jesus replied:

> Blessed are you, Simon son of Jonah, for this was not revealed to you by man, but by my Father in heaven. And I tell you that you are Peter, and on this rock I will build my church, and the gates of Hades will not overcome it. I will give you the keys of the kingdom of heaven; whatever you bind on earth will be bound in heaven, and whatever you loose on earth will be loosed in heaven (Matt. 16:17-19).

Though Peter vocally denied Jesus, all His apostles forsook Him during His trials. But Peter, like the others, was forgiven and restored. After receiving the promised power of the Holy Spirit, Peter boldly preached a sermon in Jerusalem which resulted in 3,000 Jews converting to Christ (Acts 2). God authenticated Peter's ministry with miracles and deliverances from prison and death (Acts 4; 5; 12).

About 62, Peter wrote the first letter bearing his name to strengthen Christians throughout the Roman Empire who were suffering persecution. Just before his death between 64 and 66, Peter's second letter to scattered believers warned them of false teachings creeping into Christian assemblies. The "big fisherman" (as he is affectionately dubbed by J.D. Douglas) penned eight chapters of the New Testament in two books—1 and 2 Peter.

When Peter was sentenced to die by crucifixion at the

order of Emperor Nero in Rome, he asked that his cross be turned upside down since he felt unworthy to die a death so similar to his Lord's. His wish was granted.

Jude—Brother of James and Jesus

Jude introduces himself as "a servant of Jesus Christ and a brother of James" (Jude 1:1). His later reference to the apostles shows he didn't consider himself to be one (1:17). The traditional view is that Jude is a half brother of Jesus, also called Judas (Matt. 13:55), and a carpenter by trade.

Like his older brother James, Jude didn't believe Jesus was God until after He rose from the dead.

Jude's one-chapter book is a literary classic in describing the treachery of false teachers.

> These men are blemishes at your love feasts, eating with you without the slightest qualm—shepherds who feed only themselves. They are clouds without rain, blown along by the wind; autumn trees, without fruit and uprooted—twice dead. They are wild waves of the sea, foaming up their shame; wandering stars, for whom blackest darkness has been reserved forever. Enoch, the seventh from Adam, prophesied about these men: "See, the Lord is coming with thousands upon thousands of his holy ones to judge everyone, and to convict all the ungodly of all the ungodly acts they have done in the ungodly way, and of all the harsh words ungodly sinners have spoken against him." These men are grumblers and faultfinders; they follow their own evil desires; they boast about themselves and flatter others for their own advantage (Jude 12-16).

Since Jude quotes from Peter's second letter, it was obviously written after it, probably between 66 and 80.

John—The Beloved Apostle

This Jewish fisherman from Bethsaida and Capernaum wrote 50 chapters (1,414 verses) of the New Testament in 5 books: the Gospel of John, 1 John, 2 John, 3 John, and the Revelation. His favorite reference to himself is as "the disciple whom Jesus loved" (John 13:23).

John, along with his partners, willingly forsook a profitable fishing business with his father Zebedee to follow Christ as a disciple and later as one of the 12 Apostles (Mark 1:20). Along with Peter and James, John was closer to Christ than the other nine, making him an eyewitness to more events in Jesus' entire ministry from His baptism to the ascension (John 21:24-25). The same trio later became pillars of the Jerusalem church (Gal. 2:9).

The author of the fourth Gospel stated his purpose near the end of his book: "Jesus did many other miraculous signs in the presence of His disciples, which are not recorded in this book. But these are written that you may believe that Jesus is the Christ, the Son of God, and that by believing, you may have life in His name" (John 20:30-31).

Writing the most universally appealing summary of Jesus' life, John selected seven miracles and seven claims of Christ as proofs. John wrote his Gospel after the other three, sometime between 60 and 90.

Traditions agree John went to Asia just before Jerusalem's destruction in 70. While John served as a missionary in and around Ephesus, tradition says God spared him from an attempted poisoning. His first letter, 1 John, was probably directed to the same audience as his later Revelation with clear tests of what it means to live in fellowship with God.

Two additional letters bearing his name followed soon after the first about 90—both regarding itinerant Bible teachers. Second John warns against helping false teachers, while 3 John advocates hosting true ones. Scholars still debate whether these two letters are to individuals or to churches under symbolic names.

Banished to the barren Island of Patmos, John there wrote the climax of the Bible, the Book of Revelation, originally to seven churches clustered around Ephesus in John's ministry region.

John's close disciple Polycarp in turn trained Irenaeus,

making three generations of writers directly linked to Jesus' ministry. Irenaeus says John lived until the time of Roman Emperor Trajan (98–117).

The Ultimate Proof

Seven of the eight major authors of the New Testament were voluntary martyrs for Christ. Such was also the fate of 10 of the original 12 Apostles. Their only "crime" was believing and preaching that Jesus Christ was God come in a human body. If they would recant and curse Christ, they could have been freed.

Andrew was ordered crucified on an X-shaped cross in Achaia, Greece by Governor Aepeas, enraged after his wife and brother became Christians. Bartholomew Nathanael was flayed alive with sharp knives in India as a foreign missionary. James, John's brother, was beheaded by King Herod to please the Jews. The younger James, Alphaeus' son, was crucified in Egypt and his body sawn in pieces. Judas (Jude) Thaddeus was killed with arrows at Ararat after a successful evangelistic ministry in Mesopotamia and Turkey. Philip was hanged in Heiropolis and his body wrapped in papyrus and burned. Simon the Zealot was crucified. After preaching in Partia and Persia, Thomas was killed with a spear near Madras, India.

Each refused an "easy" escape of renouncing his allegiance to Christ as Saviour and Lord.

Can there be any doubt about how convinced they were regarding the truthfulness of their message? They were willing to seal their writings with their own blood.

How convinced are *you* that Jesus is God and that the New Testament records of Him are reliable?

THE NEW TESTAMENT AUTHORS
(Chart 9)
(listed in chronological order, starting with the earliest)

AUTHOR	WRITINGS	# CHS.	OCCUPATION(S)	NATIONALITY
James	James	5	carpenter, Jesus' brother	Jew
Paul	Galatians	6	Jewish defender, Pharisee, tent-maker, apostle, foreign missionary	Jew, Roman citizen
	1 Thessalonians	5		
	2 Thessalonians	3		
	1 Corinthians	16		
	2 Corinthians	13		
	Romans	16		
	Colossians	4		
	Ephesians	6		
	Philemon	1		
	Philippians	4		
	1 Timothy	6		
	Titus	3		
	2 Timothy	4		
Tertius	Romans 16:22	1 v.	secretary to Apostle Paul	Roman?
Matthew	Matthew	28	publican (tax collector), apostle	Jew
Luke	Luke	24	physician, Paul's companion, scientist	Greek
	Acts	28		
Peter	1 Peter	5	fisherman, apostle	Jew
	2 Peter	3		
Mark	Mark	16	servant; companion of Peter, Paul, & Barnabas; foreign missionary	Jew, Roman

AUTHOR	WRITINGS	# CHS.	OCCUPATION(S)	NATIONALITY
Jude	Jude	1	carpenter, apostle, Jesus' brother	Jew
John	John	21	fisherman, apostle	Jew
	1 John	5		
	2 John	1		
	3 John	1		
	Revelation	21		
Anonymous	Hebrews	13		Jew

WHEN AND WHERE THE NEW TESTAMENT BOOKS WERE WRITTEN
(Chart 10)

DATE	BOOK	AUTHOR	WRITTEN FROM	WRITTEN TO
45?	James	James	Jerusalem	Bithynia, Pontus, etc.
48	Galatians	Paul	Antioch	Galatia
52	1 Thessalonians	Paul	Corinth	Thessalonica
	2 Thessalonians	Paul	Corinth	Thessalonica
55	1 Corinthians	Paul	Ephesus	Corinth
	2 Corinthians	Paul	Macedonia	Corinth
55–60	Mark	Mark	Rome	Romans everywhere
55–65	Matthew	Matthew	Jerusalem?	Jews
56	Romans	Paul	Corinth	Rome
	Luke	Luke	Rome	Greeks
	Acts	Luke	Rome	Theophilus
61	Colossians	Paul	Rome	Colossae
	Ephesians	Paul	Rome	Ephesus
	Philemon	Paul	Rome	Colossae
	Philippians	Paul	Rome	Philippi
62	1 Timothy	Paul	Macedonia	Ephesus
	Titus	Paul	Macedonia	Crete
62	1 Peter	Peter	Rome?	scattered Christians
64–66	2 Peter	Peter	Rome?	scattered Christians
66–80	Jude	Jude	Unknown	?
67	2 Timothy	Paul	Rome	Ephesus
68?	Hebrews	Unknown	Unknown	?
90?	John	John	Ephesus	world
	1 John	John	Ephesus	Asia
	2 John	John	Ephesus	Asia
	3 John	John	Ephesus	Asia
95	Revelation	John	Patmos Island	Asia and world

9

A New Collection

Collecting the New Testament Books

First a basalt boulder from Oregon arrived unexpectedly; then a limestone ledge from Pennsylvania, followed by quartz from California and granite from South Dakota. From every state and many foreign countries came unordered stones addressed to the same Washington, D.C. location.

Someone puzzling over the pile discovered that two stones from different states fit together perfectly, then a third, and a fourth. Finally every stone was used without alteration to form a beautiful statue. To add or delete one piece would mar the symmetry of the finished image. What should be concluded about the "random rocks"? Someone masterminded the entire project.

There is a book with an origin as amazing as that statue. Sixty-six books were collected from a wide geographical area because people thought them to be divine. Later they saw that each contributed to a continuous story. The Bible's unity is one of the strongest evidences of its heavenly origin.

How did the New Testament come to complete the world's all-time best seller?

Having the Bible as a bound volume today obscures the fact that it is a library of 66 separately produced books, which had to be brought together.

At first the early church had no thought of a New Testament; its Bible was the well-defined Old Testament, augmented by fragments of oral and written accounts of Jesus' words and works by eyewitnesses. The early church used the same Old Testament in their services with the same authority as the Jews in their synagogues at the time.

The New Testament books originated as letters to churches or individuals, spanning 1,700 miles from Jerusalem to Rome, each hand-carried by a messenger traveling on foot, animal, or wind-driven ship. Because books were scarce in those days (each copy being hand-produced), they were read at public gatherings of believers, then shared with other churches. At first, original documents were passed around; later each congregation made copies to retain for teaching, reading, and reference.

Apostolic Authority

The Lord Jesus Christ "preconfirmed" the authority of the New Testament, promising:

> The Counselor, the Holy Spirit, whom the Father will send in my name, will teach you all things and will remind you of everything I have said to you. . . . I have much more to say to you, more than you can now bear. But when He, the Spirit of truth, comes, He will guide you into all truth. He will not speak on His own; He will speak only what He hears, and He will tell you what is yet to come. He will bring glory to me by taking from what is mine and making it known to you (John 14:26; 16:12-14).

Not only would the Holy Spirit help Jesus' Apostles to accurately recall everything He had said and done, but He would also reveal correct prophecies to them. Christians believe the completed New Testament fulfills these promises.

The apostles were conscious of recording God's words, though they didn't always understand them (1 Cor. 2:13; 2 Peter 3:15-16). Eighty-seven times the apostles spoke "the word of God" (equivalent to the prophets' phrase "thus says the Lord"). They freely admitted that they wrote at God's command. Dr. Luke says of the apostles, "After they prayed, the place where they were meeting was shaken. And they were all filled with the Holy Spirit and spoke the word of God boldly" (Acts 4:31). The aged apostle John introduces the last book of the New Testament, saying:

I, John, your brother and companion in the suffering and kingdom and patient endurance that are ours in Jesus, was on the island of Patmos because of the word of God and the testimony of Jesus. On the Lord's Day I was in the Spirit, and I heard behind me a loud voice like a trumpet, which said: "Write on a scroll what you see and send it to the seven churches." (Rev. 1:9-11)

The Apostle Paul, author of nearly half of the New Testament, clearly claimed to be writing words given him by God:

When I came to you, brothers, I did not come with eloquence or superior wisdom as I proclaimed to you the testimony about God. For I resolved to know nothing while I was with you except Jesus Christ and Him crucified. I came to you in weakness and fear, and with much trembling. My message and my preaching were not with wise and persuasive words, but with a demonstration of the Spirit's power, so that your faith might not rest on men's wisdom, but on God's power. We do, however, speak a message of wisdom among the mature, but not the wisdom of this age or of the rulers of this age, who are coming to nothing. No, we speak of God's secret wisdom, a wisdom that has been hidden and that God destined for our glory before time began. None of the rulers of this age understood it, for if they had, they would not have crucified the Lord of glory. However, as it is written: "No eye has seen, no ear has heard, no mind has conceived what God has prepared for those who love Him"—but God has revealed it to us by His Spirit. The Spirit searches all things, even the deep things of God. For who among men knows the thoughts of a man except the man's spirit within him? In the same way no one knows the thoughts of God except the Spirit of God. We have not received the spirit of the world but the Spirit who is from God, that we may understand what God has freely given us. This is what we speak, not in words taught us by human wisdom but in words taught by the Spirit, expressing spiritual truths in spiritual words. The man without the Spirit does not accept the things that come from the Spirit of God, for they are foolishness to him, and he cannot understand them, because they are spiritually discerned. The spiritual man makes judgments about all things, but he himself is not subject to any man's judgment: "For who has known the mind of the Lord that he may instruct him?" But we have the mind of Christ (1 Cor. 2:1-16).

In 9 of his 13 letters, Paul introduces himself as Christ's Apostle, such as in his first letter to the Corinthian church, "Paul, called to be an apostle of Christ Jesus by the will of God" (1 Cor. 1:1). A New Testament Apostle was a position in the church equivalent with the prophets in the Old Testament. "I want you to recall the words spoken in the past by the holy prophets and the command given by our Lord and Saviour through your apostles" (2 Peter 3:2).

Peter equated his and Paul's letters (more than half of the New Testament) with Old Testament Scripture and stated that Paul wrote with God's wisdom:

Bear in mind that our Lord's patience means salvation, just as our dear brother Paul also wrote you with the wisdom that God gave him. He writes the same way in all his letters, speaking in them of these matters. His letters contain some things that are hard to understand, which ignorant and unstable people distort, as they do the other Scriptures, to their own destruction (2 Peter 3:15-16).

The apostles expected their writings to be obeyed as authoritative, because Christ was speaking through them:

I already gave you a warning when I was with you the second time. I now repeat it while absent: On my return I will not spare those who sinned earlier or any of the others, since you are demanding proof that Christ is speaking through me. He is not weak in dealing with you, but is powerful among you. . . . This is why I write these things when I am absent, that when I come I may not have to be harsh in my use of authority—the authority the Lord gave me for building you up, not for tearing you down (2 Cor. 13:2-3, 10).

Disobeying an apostle of God brought severe penalties. "If anyone does not obey our instruction in this letter, take special note of him. Do not associate with him, in order that he may feel ashamed" (2 Thes. 3:14). Paul claimed his message was authoritative, because it came directly from God; anyone who contradicted it should be eternally condemned.

But even if we or an angel from heaven should preach a Gospel other than the one we preached to you, let him be eternally condemned! As we have already said, so now I say again: If anybody is preaching to you a Gospel other than what you accepted, let him be eternally condemned! Am I now trying to win the approval of men, or of God? Or am I trying to please men? If I were still trying to please men, I would not be a servant of Christ. I want you to know, brothers, that the Gospel I preached is not something that man made up. I did not receive it from any man, nor was I taught it;

rather, I received it by revelation from Jesus Christ (Gal. 1:8-12).

As with the Old Testament prophets, God confirmed the apostles' message by supernatural signs. "Everyone was filled with awe, and many wonders and miraculous signs were done by the apostles" (Acts 2:43).

> How shall we escape if we ignore such a great salvation? This salvation, which was first announced by the Lord, was confirmed to us by those who heard him. God also testified to it by signs, wonders and various miracles, and gifts of the Holy Spirit distributed according to His will (Heb. 2:3-4).

Contemporary Confirmations

The Apostles' contemporaries received their writings as authoritative. No time lapse was needed, nor any action of a church council. From the very beginning, the early church "devoted themselves to the apostles' teaching" (Acts 2:42).

When Paul wrote to Timothy, "For the Scripture says, 'Do not muzzle the ox while it is treading out the grain,' and 'The worker deserves his wages,'" he quoted from Deuteronomy and Luke in the same sentence, calling them both equal Scripture (1 Tim. 5:18, quoting Deut. 25:4 and Luke 10:7). Deuteronomy 25:4 says, "Do not muzzle an ox while it is treading out the grain," while Luke 10:7 states, "Stay in that house, eating and drinking whatever they give you, for the worker deserves his wages. Do not move around from house to house."

Jude quotes from Peter as an authoritative word from God (Jude 18; 2 Peter 3:3). Peter placed his and the other apostolic writings on a par with the sacred Old Testament writings (2 Peter 3:1-2).

As soon as a book's authenticity was verified by apostolic signature or delivery by a reliable apostolic messenger, it was read to the congregation. Accepted books must have been written by an apostle or someone closely associated with an apostle. Papias (a disciple of the Apostle John) said Mark wrote the second Gospel as a scribe for Peter, and Justyn Martyr (a mid-second-century Christian writer) asserted Luke wrote his two letters to Theophilus (Luke and Acts) for Paul. Both Peter and Paul acknowledged using secretaries (1 Peter 5:12; Rom. 16:22).

Apostles had special authority as eyewitnesses of Christ who were commissioned as His spokesmen (Mark 3:14; Acts 1:21-22). New Testament apostles are equated with Old Testament prophets (Rev. 22:9). After forming the foundation of the church, apostles were guaranteed a prominent place in Christ's kingdom (Luke 22:29-30; Eph. 2:19-20).

Making Collections

The *canon* (the list of books accepted as inspired and included in the Bible) was actually completed when John wrote the last book about 95. But it took time for the New Testament books sent to diverse locations to be collected and universally accepted.

Before the close of the first century, Paul's letters were circulated as a collection titled, *The Apostle,* its parts labeled, "To the Romans" and so on. Not long after John wrote his Revelation, the four Gospels were brought into one group called, *The Gospel,* each of its four parts titled, "According to Matthew," etc.

Because collections of books were made at different times and places, their contents were not always the same. Each location didn't have copies of all the same books yet. The limited circulation of a few books helps explain why they were later questioned by some. Christianity was a far-flung international religion without the benefit of a central temple where the sacred scrolls were stored.

By the end of the first century, all New Testament books were accepted as divine by believers somewhere. No writing of an apostle was knowingly rejected by the church, nor has any apostolic book been proven to be lost.

The letter from Laodicea mentioned in Colossians 4:16 may be Ephesians, whose name is missing from Ephesians

1:1 in many Greek manuscripts. But there is no problem with Bible prophets and apostles writing books and letters which have not been preserved. God has preserved those writings which have timeless and universal value.

External Evidences

The earliest translations of the Greek New Testament were into the Aramaic and Latin languages, for the Syrians and Romans, respectively. The Syriac version (called the Peshitta) became the Bible of the eastern churches and was later translated into Arabic, Persian, and Armenian.

The Old Latin version became the Bible of the western churches and for a thousand years was the source of most other translations. Jerome's Latin Vulgate version, made from the Old Latin about 400, became the official Bible of the Roman Catholic Church.

Both these early versions were made in the second century, about 50 years after John wrote his Revelation, and testify that the New Testament as we know it was completely compiled by that time.

The church fathers (church leaders living from about 80 to 180) viewed the apostles as a fixed group with a now finished work. These extrabiblical authors who were closest to the apostles claimed to be far beneath them, equating the apostles' words with the words of Christ himself. Within a generation after John, all 27 books of the New Testament were cited as Scripture by some church leader. Within 200 years, all but 11 verses of the New Testament were quoted in more than 36,000 citations of the church fathers that have been preserved.

The church fathers were well educated and voluminous writers. Clement refers to Matthew, Luke, Romans, Corinthians, Hebrews, 1 Timothy, and 1 Peter. Ignatius called the Gospels "the words of Jesus." Polycarp, a disciple of the Apostle John, quoted from two-thirds of the New Testament books in a short letter. Though Irenaeus quoted from the New Testament over 1,800 times, Tertullian holds the record with 7,200 New Testament quotes in his writings.

Making Copies of Copies

Like the Hebrew Old Testament, all copies of the New Testament before the fifteenth century were handwritten.

Over 4,000 copies of these Greek-language manuscripts exist today. Since the original manuscripts and early copies of it were written on papyrus, very few manuscripts have survived in this fragile form.

Among the oldest of these are the John Ryland's Fragment (part of John from about 130), Bodmer Papyrus II (most of John from about 150), and the Chester Beatty Papyrii (most of the New Testament from about 200). The oldest of all may be parts of the New Testament in the Dead Sea Scrolls collection. If Spanish papyriologist Dr. José O'Callaghan's work proves true, parts of several New Testament books exist from within a decade or two of their origin!

Vellum, made from specially-smoothed and dried calf skin, was used for most copies from the fourth century onward, so more copies have survived in this more durable form. The oldest complete copies of the New Testament in Greek are Codex Sinaiticus (fourth century, discovered at St. Catherine's Monastery at Mt. Sinai) and Codex Alexandrinus (fifth century, mentioned previously as also containing most of the Old Testament). Most of the New Testament is contained in Codex Vaticanus (fourth century, at the Vatican Library in Rome) and Codex Ephraemi (fifth century).

Hundreds, perhaps thousands, of biblical manuscripts were destroyed by the Romans when Emperor Diocletian ordered the destruction of all "the sacred writings of the Christians" in 303.

The Big Three Agree

For several centuries after Christ, Christians reverenced the same New Testament we have today, basing their lifestyle and worship on it. There was no question about the authenticity of the collection for several centuries.

The three major branches of Christendom (Greek Orthodox, Protestant, and Roman Catholic) agree on the New Testament's 27 books as *Scripture* ("sacred writings"), completing God's written revelation to mankind.

Other religious writings appeared while the New Testament was being formed, the Epistle of Barnabas (not by the Barnabas of Acts) and the Shepherd of Hermas (an allegory by a Roman Christian) being two of the most popular. Yet these books were never received as equal to apostolic writings. About 170, the Muratorian document (named for its discoverer) said the Shepherd could be read in Christian meetings, but was not to be counted among the prophetic (Old Testament) or apostolic (New Testament) writings.

Some books with false claims of authorship ("pseudepigraphic") attempted to fill gaps in the sacred record, such as Jesus' childhood years, portraying him as a temperamental child who would kill a playmate or give life to a clay pigeon on a whim. No church leader or council ever accepted these books, which emphasize miracles over teaching and are quite different from Scripture in purpose and content. Eusebius, a fourth century Greek scholar and Bible copier, called them "totally absurd and impious."

As time went on, Christians desired an official list of sacred books. They wanted to standardize what should be read as God's words and determine which books to translate in foreign missions. They also wanted to be certain which books were worth dying for. Some believers handed over other religious writings, hoping the Roman soldiers wouldn't know the difference, but they considered it a denial of the faith to surrender New Testament Scriptures for destruction.

Long after their original acceptance, several New Testament books were questioned. Later all questions were resolved. Hebrews and 2 and 3 John were suspect to some because they were anonymous. Hebrews was popularly ascribed to Paul and claims divine authority regardless of its human author (2:2-4). Earliest tradition as well as style clearly marks 2 and 3 John, as well as the fourth Gospel and his first letter (1 John) which were also unsigned, as the Apostle John's.

James was questioned because its emphasis on works

seemed incompatible with Paul's stress on faith. Yet, Paul also emphasizes that faith in God will show itself in good works (Eph. 2:8-9; Titus 3:8).

The style of 2 Peter is different from that of 1 Peter, yet both claim to be from Peter. Not only is the subject matter different in the two letters, but Peter used a secretary in his first letter and not in his second.

Jude was a problem to some because it quoted Enoch, an apocryphal (false) book. Jude, though quoting pagan sources, does not commend them; Paul does the same in Titus 1:12.

Because it was used by a cult, Revelation became suspect. The misuse of Revelation by a cult did not weaken its authority, which was based on the authorship of John the Apostle (Rev. 1:4).

Knowing such questions were thoughtfully discussed and resolved makes us more certain that the right books were included in the New Testament.

Is 27 The Right Number?

About 200, Tertullian (leader of the Carthage church) first used the term "New Testament," recognizing its inspiration as equal to the books of Genesis through Malachi. Justin Martyr said the "memoirs of the Apostles" were read in Christian gatherings on Sundays along with the "writings of the Prophets" (the Old Testament).

In 367, Athanasius (leader of the Alexandrian church) published the first known list that matches perfectly with the Bible's 66 books as we have them today. Jerome recognized the same collection in his Latin Vulgate. Augustine also defined the New Testament canon as its current 27 books.

Two North African church councils (at Hippo in 385 and Carthage in 397) definitively declared the Bible complete in the 66 books in today's Protestant Bibles. Their action didn't confer any authority on the New Testament; it only ratified what was already the accepted practice of the churches. The New Testament and the church grew up together.

Many religious groups seek to justify their modern existence by claiming to have received a revelation from God
subsequent and superior to the Bible. But Jesus said the
apostles' teaching would be the basis on which others
would believe in Him (John 17:20). God has once and for
all delivered the faith to His saints through Christ's apostles
in the first century (Jude 3, 17). The Bible is a collection of
authorized books flowing from the mind of God through the
pens and personalities of His prophets and apostles.

More could have been written about Jesus—enough to
smother the world with books. But what was selected for
the Scriptures is sufficient for anyone to believe that Jesus is
the Christ, the Son of God, and to receive eternal life
through His name (John 20:30-31; 21:25).

The last Bible book opens with a blessing for those who
read, hear, and take to heart its words, and closes with a
curse on anyone who would add to it or subtract from it.

> Blessed is the one who reads the words of this prophecy,
> and blessed are those who hear it and take to heart what
> is written in it, because the time is near (Rev. 1:3).

> I warn everyone who hears the words of the prophecy
> of this book: If anyone adds anything to them, God will
> add to him the plagues described in this book. And if
> anyone takes words away from this book of prophecy,
> God will take away from him his share in the tree of life
> and in the holy city, which are described in this book
> (Rev. 22:18-19).

The Scheme Of Things

Like the Greek version of the Old Testament, the New Testament books are topically arranged. After 4 Gospels about
the life of Christ, the Book of Acts summarizes the establish-
ment and expansion of the church throughout the Roman
Empire. Twenty-one letters to churches or members of
them follow, the first 13 by the Apostle Paul all named for
the church or person addressed. The remaining 8 by others

are largely named for the sender. One book of prophecy, the Revelation, closes the collection and the whole canon of sacred Scripture. See Chart 11 for the New Testament books listed topically.

THE NEW TESTAMENT TOPICAL ARRANGEMENT
(Chart 11)

HISTORY	LETTERS	PROPHECY
History of Christ (Gospels)	From Paul to Churches	27 Revelation
1 Matthew	6 Romans	
2 Mark	7 1 Corinthians	
3 Luke	8 2 Corinthians	
4 John	9 Galatians	
	10 Ephesians	
History of Church	11 Philippians	
5 Acts	12 Colossians	
	13 1 Thessalonians	
	14 2 Thessalonians	
	From Paul to Pastors	
	15 1 Timothy	
	16 2 Timothy	
	17 Titus	
	18 Philemon	
	From Others	
	19 Hebrews	
	20 James	
	21 1 Peter	
	22 2 Peter	
	23 1 John	
	24 2 John	
	25 3 John	
	26 Jude	

10

Old English Originals

Putting the Bible into English

When the old original tintype of beloved great grandfather Hamilton began to fade and yellow, Sharon had a photo lab make an enlarged restoration copy of the original. Is the copy now on Sharon's mantle actually a photograph of great granddad Hamilton? Not really; it's only a copy of one. But it's such a careful reproduction that she can rightly refer to it as a photo of her great grandfather.

In a similar way, the Bible in the English language may be referred to as the Word of God. True, it's only a copy and in a different language than the original. But it has been made with such extreme care to conform to the original that for all practical purposes it can be referred to as the same Scriptures that were originally produced by 50 people in Greek, Hebrew, and Aramaic and hand-copied for centuries!

Early English Versions
Through the influence of the Roman Empire, Latin became the official language of the Roman Catholic Church. Commissioned by the Bishop of Rome in 383, Jerome spent 25

years making a Latin Bible for the common people. Hence, his version is called the Latin Vulgate (from *vulgar,* meaning "common"). Already a renowned grammarian, Jerome went to Bethlehem to study Hebrew under a Jewish rabbi and to make use of old biblical manuscripts.

Here is the beginning of the "Lord's Prayer" in Latin, *"Pater noster, qui es in coelis, sanctificetur nomen tuum. Adveniat regnum tuum; fiat voluntas tua, ut in coelo, ita etiam in terra"* (Matt. 6:9-10). For interesting comparisons, this same passage will be quoted below for some later versions.

For a thousand years, Jerome's Latin Bible reigned supreme as *the* Bible version. But with the demise of the Roman Empire, Europe's beginning emergence from the dark Middle Ages, and England's ascendancy as the major world power, by the fourteenth century people were becoming dissatisfied with church services in a language few could understand, and they clamored for a translation of the Bible in plain English.

A few parts of the Bible had previously been translated into early English (called Anglo-Saxon), a language almost impossible to understand today without special study. Bede, an English historian of the eighth century, started to translate the Vulgate into English because only scholars could understand Latin. Legend says Bede died as he finished his translation of John's Gospel in 735. Here is how the Lord's prayer begins in early Anglo-Saxon, *"Uren fader dhic art in heofnas, sic gehalyed dhin noma, to cymedh dhin ric, sic dhin willa sue in heofnas and in eardhs."*

Can you decipher it better in later Anglo-Saxon? *"Faeder ure thaet the eart on heofenum, Si thin nama gehalgod, To becume thin rice."*

But it would be another 650 years before the English-speaking world would have a Bible in its language.

In the fourteenth century, John Wycliffe sent out poor priests called Lollards to preach to the people in their own language instead of the Latin used in the churches. Wycliffe championed social and religious reforms in his native England, maintaining that every person should be able to read the Bible and "learn the words of the Gospel according to its simplicity."

In 1380 John Wycliffe produced a homely, forthright English version of the New Testament from the Latin, followed by the Old Testament two years later. For the first time, the entire Bible was available in English. Wycliffe's is the first complete translation of the Bible in English and is also the first modern English version. Though it has many spelling differences and a number of archaic words, Wycliffe's Bible is reasonably easy to understand even today. *"Our fader that art in heuenas, halewid be thi name, thi kingdom comme to, be thi wille done as in heuen so in erthe."*

Because Wycliffe's translation could only be produced by hand, copies were scarce and expensive. But his work was so highly valued that people would pay well for the privilege of reading from a copy. Because Wycliffe translated from the Latin, making a version of a version, his work has no special value for accuracy.

Wycliffe adopted the chapter divisions created by Stephen Langdon in 1227 and used in all Bible versions since. At first, the Hebrew and Greek texts had no divisions, not even spaces between the words. So the Bible had been completed for over 1,100 years before chapter divisions as we know them were introduced into the text. Though helpful for reference, they sometimes occur at unfortunate places (such as between chapters 15 and 16 of 1 Corinthians) and often cause people to read the Scriptures in artificial segments. Many of the Bible books were letters or sermons designed to be read at one sitting.

John Wycliffe, the "Morning Star of the Reformation," paved the way for the later Protestant reformers, but died before Roman and Anglican persecution broke out against English versions of the Bible. In 1408 English subjects were forbidden to make or read a version of the Bible in their native tongue. After Wycliffe was posthumously condemned as a heretic, his body was exhumed and burned.

Gutenberg's invention of movable type in Mainz, Germany about 1450 made the printing of books possible and economical. The first book to be printed on the new press was the Latin Bible. By the turn of the century, the Bible had been printed in 14 languages.

In 1516 a milestone was reached in the Bible's story when the great monk-scholar Erasmus published the first printed edition of the New Testament in Greek. Now scholars everywhere could have access to the same text of the New Testament in its original language. A later edition of Erasmus' Greek text formed the basis of what has become known as the "Received Text" because of a printer's preface stating this is the text received from the beginning. The Latin equivalent, "Textus Receptus" or the "TR," are still common names for the fifth edition of Erasmus' Greek text.

The Protestant Reformation was awakening the masses to personal reading and studying of the Scriptures with the subsequent demand for copies easy to read and understand by the average layperson.

Martin Luther realized his Reformation needed a Bible in the language of the people, so in 1534 he made the first European Bible based on the original Hebrew and Greek instead of the Latin. His German version of the Lord's prayer begins, *"Vater unser, der du bist im himmel, geheiliget werde dein name. Dein reich komme, dein wille geschehe wie im himmel auch auf erden."*

The Father of the English Bible

Oxford and Cambridge scholar William Tyndale desired to translate the Scriptures into English from the original languages, vowing to an Anglican opponent, "If God spare my life, ere many years I will cause a boy that driveth the plow shall know more of the Scriptures than thou doest."

Since state church authorities in England prohibited an English version, Tyndale translated in Germany, using Erasmus' Greek text as the basis for his New Testament translation. In 1526, when copies of his finished work began to be smuggled into England in shipments of grain and cloth, church leaders burned confiscated copies in public ceremonies.

William Tyndale is called the "Father of the English Bible" because his was the first English translation from the original languages instead of the Latin. It was also the first English translation of the Bible to ever be printed on a press. So well done was Tyndale's work that it forms the base for the King James Version (KJV) and nearly every English version up to and including the English Revised Version of 1881 and the American Standard Version of 1901.

The KJV is really an updated fifth revision of Tyndale's translation, preserving many words he coined, such as "peacemaker," "passover," "scapegoat," and "longsuffering." Tyndale made a version for the common man, using "congregation" for "church," "repentance" for "penance," "love" for "charity," etc.

Using the English of his day, Tyndale's Lord's Prayer begins, "O oure Father which arte in heuenas, halowed by thy name. Lett thy kyngdo come. Thy wyll be fulfillet, even in erth, as hit ys in heuen."

Betrayed by "friends," Tyndale was imprisoned while working on his version of the Old Testament. A letter has survived which he wrote to a prison official. After asking for the kindness of a warmer cap and coat, Tyndale writes,

> My overcoat is worn out; my shirts are also worn out. . . . And I ask to be allowed to have a lamp in the evening; it is indeed wearisome sitting alone in the dark. But most of all, I beg and beseech . . . that he will kindly permit me to have the Hebrew Bible, Hebrew grammar, and Hebrew dictionary, that I may pass the time in that study.

His requests ignored, Tyndale was found guilty of heresy, strangled, and burned on a stake near Brussels, Belgium, in 1535. His dying prayer, "Lord, open Thou the King of England's eyes," was answered just four years later.

Tyndale didn't live to complete his version of the Old Testament, a task continued by Miles Coverdale, who also fled to Germany from England. Coverdale's Bible was the first complete English Bible to be printed on a press in 1535.

Incorporating Matthew's 1537 Bible into his work, Coverdale in 1539 produced the Great Bible, so called because of its large size designed for church display. King Henry VIII authorized every church building in England to be given a copy just four years after Tyndale was killed for the "crime" of making an English translation! Preachers sometimes complained about parishoners remaining in the foyer to read the Bible instead of attending services.

Coverdale's Psalms are still included in the Anglican Book of Common Prayer. The later, Geneva, Bishops', and KJV Bibles were all based on the Great Bible, the culmination of Tyndale's work.

The Most Popular Bible of the Sixteenth Century
The Geneva Bible was produced by English Puritans in Geneva, Switzerland, in 1560 under the auspices of reformers John Calvin and John Knox. Protestant persecutions under England's Queen Mary ("bloody Mary") caused many Christians to migrate to freedom and safety in Geneva.

The first English Bible mass-produced in a convenient size with illustrations and commentary, this excellent translation became very popular with the common people. But the Geneva Bible was opposed by both governmental and ecclesiastical authorities because of its caustic marginal notes.

This was the first English version to incorporate modern verse divisions, printing each verse as a separate paragraph. Robert Stephanus is credited with creating biblical verse divisions between 1551 and 1555.

Words not found in the original but supplied for meaning's sake were indicated in italics. It was also the first to be printed in the more easily readable modern Roman type, previous ones being in Old English or "black letter" typefaces.

Sometimes dubbed the "Breeches Bible" for its translation of Genesis 3:7, "Adam and Eve sewed fig leaves together, and made themselves breeches," the Geneva Bible was the one Shakespeare used. When the Puritans came to America, this is the version they brought, for the KJV was too new and had not yet gained wide acceptance.

In reaction to the Geneva Bible, the Bishops' Bible was released in 1568 as the "authorized" version to be used in churches. Similar to the former, it, of course, deleted the Reformers' notes.

The Greatest English Version

The controversies over the extant Bibles prompted church leaders to convene at Hampton Court, a London royal residence. Their proposal of a new Bible acceptable to all caused King James I of England in 1604 to authorize a new translation of the Bible, which would be published seven years later as the King James Version. The resolution accepted by king and committee stated:

> that a translation be made of the whole Bible, as consonant as can be to the original Hebrew and Greek; and this to be set out and printed, without any marginal notes, and only to be used in all Churches in England in time of divine service.

Fifty-four scholars were appointed to make the new version, using all known copies of the original manuscripts and the Bishops' Bible (a revision of Tyndale's work) as the base. Their translation process was the most thorough of any work before or since. The committee was organized into six different groups to translate given Scripture sections. Each group's work was submitted to all five of the other groups. A committee of six (one per group) had the final say.

Despite the great variety of men on the team (their only qualification being "proficient as Bible scholars"), the final product is unparalleled in harmonious style and beauty. Its smooth-flowing Old English has a majesty unmatched by any other version. Dedicated to its sponsoring sovereign, the work became known as the "Authorized" or "King James Version" of the Bible.

The first 1611 printing was a large church edition like the Bishops' Bible it replaced.

John Blaney updated the KJV in 1769, and his is the version of the KJV in common use today. "Our Father which art in heaven, hallowed be thy name. Thy kingdom come. Thy will be done in earth, as it is in heaven."

Though the KJV now uses some archaic expressions, it is doubtful if any other English version will ever replace it among the masses. The KJV still remains the all-time best-selling Bible.

The KJV has been updated in such editions as the *New King James Version* (NKJV) and the *New Scofield Reference Bible*. About 300 words that have changed greatly over the 300 years since the KJV was produced have been done for modernization. "Conversation" was changed to "behavior"; "prevent" to "precede"; "suffer" to "allow," to mention a few.

Several printed editions of the KJV over the centuries show that scribes writing by hand weren't the only ones to make copying errors. A 1631 edition was called the "Wicked Bible" because it omitted "not" from the seventh commandment. The "Murderer's Bible" (1795) misspelled "filled" as "killed" in Mark 7:27. The "Vinegar Bible" substituted "vinegar" for "vineyard" for the Luke 20 parable. The "Bug Bible" printed a line of Psalm 91 as, "Thou shalt not be afraid of any bugges by night."

Roman Catholic Versions

Worldwide, the official Roman Catholic Church version still remains Jerome's Latin Vulgate from the fourth century. But an authorized English translation of the New Testament from the Latin was produced in 1582 in Rheims, France, followed in 1610 by the Old Testament at Douai, France. Because they came from the same era, both the Douai-Rheims and the KJV use similar Elizabethan English. Bishop Challoner revised the Douai-Rheims (named after its cities of origin) in 1750.

The next major English Catholic version didn't come till

1941, when the Confraternity New Testament appeared, based on the Vulgate but influenced by Greek manuscripts. The companion Old Testament of 1952 was the first Roman Catholic version to be based on original language manuscripts.

When a new version of the New Testament based on the Greek text was produced in 1970 and the Old Testament extensively revised, the Confraternity Version was renamed *The New American Bible*. Today this is the only English version authorized for use in liturgy and the mass by Roman Catholic churches in the United States.

The Jerusalem Bible, translated from the French (1961), is basically literal yet contemporary, but contains theologically liberal notes. This is the authorized English version for Canadian Catholic churches. In 1965 a specially altered edition of the *Revised Standard Version* (RSV) was officially endorsed by Catholics. It changed references to Jesus' "brothers" to "brethren," for example. Special editions of the *Good News Bible* and other versions have also been approved for Catholics' personal use.

Bridges to Our Era
For nearly 300 years the KJV reigned supreme among English-speaking Protestants everywhere. Four major factors influenced an explosion of English translations in the last 100 years. Gutenberg's press and the Protestant Reformation have already been mentioned.

A third stimulus came in the form of new biblical manuscript discoveries, especially three fifth-century Bibles in Greek—Codices Alexandrinus, Sinaiticus, and Vaticanus—and later the Dead Sea Scrolls. Though all manuscript finds have provided overwhelming confirmation of the accuracy of the biblical text's preservation, there are some differences among the manuscripts. The majority of manuscripts are in the "family" of those used by Erasmus' Greek text, the basis for the KJV and its English predecessors.

Englishmen B.F. Westcott and A.J. Hort developed an elaborate procedure for categorizing and evaluating Greek biblical manuscripts. Their "critical" Greek text, eclectically produced in 1881 from all the extant manuscripts, sounds good in theory, except many feel they gave far too much prominence to the three fifth-century manuscripts. As a result, their Greek text eliminated over 200 passages from the majority text and altered about 6,000 others.

Today a controversy still exists over which Greek text is the proper basis for the New Testament. The more commonly used shorter edition begun by Westcott and Hort is continuously being revised as *Nestle's Greek New Testament*. Most English versions since 1881 have been made from this eclectic text. But modern scholarship has seriously challenged Westcott and Hort's underlying theory.

Older does not necessarily mean better for ancient manuscripts, for the fifth-century ones may be less accurate copies than those from 600 years later in a different part of the world which represent copies of purer texts. The places and means of discovery of the fifth-century manuscripts make them suspect for some. Were they originally kept out of use because they were faulty? And why were they all secreted away by the Roman Church until recent times?

Even with the great flood of biblical manuscript discoveries in the last century, Erasmus' Greek text still stands as the best representative of the majority of them. Those who have held steadfastly to Erasmus' larger traditional majority text (the basis for the KJV) may be proven right after all!

After 250 years the first new English translation was made since the KJV. The English Revised Version (ERV) of 1881 (New Testament) and 1885 (Old Testament) was the first to use the new critical, eclectic text of Westcott and Hort. One hundred scholars from England and America were involved, reviewing each passage five times.

Hailed as an epochal event, the entire text of the ERV New Testament was published in special editions of the *Chicago Tribune* and *Chicago Sun Times* on May 22, 1881, simultaneous with the version's release in New York.

In 1901 the ERV was published in the USA as the American Standard Version (ASV) with minor accommodations to stateside usage. The ASV has been hailed as weak in English but strong in Greek, so accurate to the original that it was widely adopted as the Bible text in Bible schools and seminaries.

The ASV was revised and published in 1946 and 1952 as the Revised Standard Version (RSV) by the National Council of Churches of Christ in America and widely promoted among their constituents. But conservative Christians castigated the new version for its seemingly liberal bias against the deity of the Lord Jesus Christ and its freeness in altering the millennia-old Masoretes' Hebrew text.

Conservatives rallied around their own edition of the ASV, published as the New American Standard Bible (NASB) in 1963 and 1971. Another conservative alternative to the RSV was *The New Berkeley Bible*, also called *The Modern Language Bible.*

The greatest flurry of translations has come in the last 30 years, prompted largely by the fourth major influence—the proliferation of Christian publishing houses, each desiring a profitable Bible to sell. Since each Bible producer copyrights its version, other publishers must pay royalties and licensing fees to use another's text. Often competitors are not given permission to use a particular Bible text for any price. To stay in business, many publishers feel they must create their own translation.

Unfortunately, we'll live to see many more new English versions, while there are still over 3,000 people groups in the world who still have *no* portion of the Word of God in their language.

The Latest Words in English

All Bible versions can be placed on a continuum between translations and paraphrases. Translations convert every word of the original Greek, Hebrew, or Aramaic into their English equivalents. They may have to change the word order to make sense, but there is a word-for-word correspondence. Paraphrases are only concerned with communicating the thought of the original.

Periphrastic versions are much more readable. They flow

along smoothly, getting the big ideas across in everyday "street" language. But their easier readability comes with an increased danger of unreliability. The more someone summarizes God's words into what he thinks God said, the more room there is for interpretative bias.

But with the greater accuracy and reliability of literal translations comes a corresponding formal, precise, "textbookish" kind of English that's harder to read and understand.

The KJV and ASV are the most literal English versions.

The Amplified Bible is an expanded literal version with definitions and extra shades of meaning from the original languages included in the text. For example, in John 3:16:

> For God so greatly loved and dearly prized the world that He [even] gave up His only begotten Son, so that whoever believes in (trusts, clings to, relies on) Him may not perish—come to destruction, be lost—but have eternal (everlasting) life.

The *Good News Bible* (GNB) is a simplified literal version with a limited vocabulary. Originally designed for people using English as a second language, it has also sold well to those raised on English, but who don't know it as well as they ought. The New Testament portion of the GNB is called *Good News for Modern Man.*

The Living Bible (TLB) is one of the all-time best-selling paraphrases. Ken Taylor began to rewrite the ASV in his own words for his children. He was soon so inundated with requests for copies, he published it. Romans grew into *Living Letters,* and finally Taylor produced the complete *Living Bible.*

It's no accident that most Bible versions fit in the middle of the translation-paraphrase continuum, because they are trying to strike a balance between accuracy and readability. A favorite version of many from the center cluster is J.B. Phillips' *New Testament in Modern English.* He began his edition to make the Bible "come more alive" to the youth group in his church. In the process many feel he produced a good "dynamic-equivalence translation," reproducing in the English reader the same effect the Greek would have had on its original readers. Phillips begins the Lord's prayer, "Our heavenly Father, may your name be honored; may your kingdom come, and your will be done on earth as it is in heaven."

For an up-to-date edition of the whole Bible which balances readability with reliability, most evangelical Christians would recommend the *New International Version* (NIV), which is becoming the most popular, in part due to the marketing savvy of its publisher, the Zondervan Corporation, and its cosponsorship by the International Bible Society.

The NIV was produced by an international team of scholars from three continents and 10 denominations. After each portion was approved by the committees of Hebrew and Greek scholars, it was submitted to literary consultants who evaluated its English style and clarity of expression.

Now many computer versions of the Bible are available, with correlated programs that enable the user to locate any and all passages on a subject in about two seconds!

In evaluating any edition of the Bible, one has to consider its intended purpose. One version may be better for private detailed study, another clearer for public reading, while yet another is better for teens or children.

Choosing and Using a Bible
A good reference/study edition of the Bible is an invaluable tool that provides helps before, during, and after the Bible text itself. All reference Bibles have introductory pages to each of the 66 Bible books, summarizing the five big W's—Who, What, When, Where, and Why. Currently, the best background pages far and away are those authored by Ken Boa and incorporated in *The Open Bible* (KJV, NKJV, or NASB, published by Thomas Nelson).

On every page of study Bible text are helpful cross-references. These are the small-print verse indications usually listed down the left or right-hand margins, but sometimes in a center column. The *Open Bible* inserts them into the text.

Cross-references are a shortcut to other Scriptures that will usually provide one or a combination of:

● the same word used in another context,

● the same event,

● the same idea from another perspective. Most cross-references add something new to the word, event, or thought in the current passage. Sometimes a reference listed with the first verse of a Bible book or chapter is meant to go with the whole book or chapter.

Many editions use a "chain" approach leading the user from one passage to another in a progressive summary of Bible doctrines or teachings about the Christian life. The best and most complete set of biblical cross-references are currently found in *The Thompson Chain Reference Bible* (KJV or NIV, published by B.B. Kirkbride and Zondervan).

At the front and back of all reference Bibles are copious pages of helpful outlines, charts, maps, histories and backgrounds of biblical subjects, etc. An outstandingly helpful tool is the 330-page "Biblical Cyclopedic Concordance" included in all editions of *The Open Bible* mentioned above.

Study Bibles also include notes of explanation or interpretation of the biblical text. The best commentaries are included in *The New Scofield Reference Bible* (NIV or updated KJV, published by Oxford and others), *The Ryrie Study Bible* (KJV or NASB, published by Moody Press), and *The NIV Study Bible* (NIV, published by Zondervan). The best life-application notes are found in *The Life-Application Bible* (TLB, published by Tyndale House) and *The Serendipity Bible* (NIV, published by Serendipity House).

As you can see, no single study Bible has the best of all components. If you already have one good leather Bible, additional volumes can be purchased in much less expensive hardback editions. Whichever version you select needs to be read, interpreted, and applied. The bottom line is listening seriously to what God is telling us through His Word. And then changing our attitudes or actions accordingly.

11

The Unfinished Book

Getting the Bible into Other Languages

At first the Bible was copied and circulated in its original languages.

The first known "foreign" edition of the Old Testament was the Septuagint. For centuries after the New Testament was added, the whole canon circulated in Greek, made a world trade language by the conquests of Alexander the Great.

But as Christianity spread to non-Greek-speaking peoples, the Scriptures were translated into other languages. The first foreign translations of the whole Bible were into Syrian and Latin. By 1500, printed translations of the Bible in German, Italian, Catalan, and Czech were added.

Tyndale's translation began an era of intense translation and Bible publication in the English language. The Geneva Bible went through 200 editions, with one or more editions every year for 56 consecutive years. The KJV in 1611 dominated the field for two-and-a-half centuries.

Luther's German translation soon became the model for translations by his followers into Danish, Swedish, Icelandic, and Finnish. Still, by 1800 only 67 languages had any part of the Scripture, with only 40 of these having the whole Bible. Most of these translations were for the established churches of Europe. Aggressive pioneer translation work awaited the European churches' awakening to a worldwide missionary vision.

Motivated by Missions
The first "modern" translation of Scripture in a non-European language for the purpose of evangelism was Matthew's Gospel in Malay by a director of the Dutch East Indies Company in 1629. The first entire Bible in a new language for missions was the work of Englishman John Eliott for use in America in 1663. Danish missionary Ziegenbalg translated the first New Testament into a language of India in 1717.

Deeply moved by reading reports of Count Zinzendorf and the Moravian missionaries, William Carey followed their example and went to India in 1793. Believing Bible translation was the most effective way to evangelize, Carey was responsible for getting the Scriptures into over 65 languages of India and Asia during the next 40 years.

Carey's work and writings resulted in the formation of 12 missionary societies in Europe and America. Beginning in 1804, Bible societies were formed to translate, publish, and distribute Scripture.

The American Bible Society, since 1815, has distributed over 4 billion Bibles in nearly 500 languages. In 1984 alone they printed and distributed 114,458,279 copies of God's Word—most for free or a modest, heavily subsidized cost.

Bible translation soon was taking place worldwide, with all or parts of the Bible published in Tahitian in Oceania (1818), Chinese (1822), Aymaran in Latin America (1829), Malagasy (1835), and Yoruba in Africa (1884). By 1870, the Malagasy Bible without missionaries resulted in a growth from handfuls to thousands of believers in thriving churches.

In the first 30 years of the nineteenth century, 86 languages received the Scriptures for the first time, more than during all 18 centuries preceding. Sixty-six of these were languages outside Europe.

Altogether, 456 languages received Scripture for the first time during the nineteenth century, 520 more in the first two quarters of the twentieth, and almost 600 more in the third quarter. By 1982, the entire Bible had been published in 279 languages, the New Testament in 551 more, and at least one book of the Bible in another 933.

That means the Scriptures have now been provided in over 1,700 different languages.

On the Current Scene

New translations continue with one or more books of the Bible now appearing in a new language every two weeks, most for missionary evangelism or newly founded churches.

Who are the people involved in the modern Bible translation movement?

The world's largest missionary organization, the Wycliffe Bible Translators (WBT), is committed to use Bible translation to fulfill the Great Commission. Over 7,000 Wycliffe translators and support workers from 34 countries (1,500 are from outside the USA) have teamed together to produce New Testaments and parts of the Old in 200 languages. They are currently working in 761 more languages spoken in 40 different countries.

WBT cofounder Cameron Townsend's missionary career began in 1917 when he went to Guatemala as a Bible distributor with the then Central American Mission. The need for Bible translation was indelibly impressed upon him when he discovered that 60 percent of Guatemala's Indian population could not speak Spanish. "What am I doing selling Spanish Bibles to people who cannot understand them," Townsend asked himself.

So with no training in linguistics (not even a college degree), Townsend settled down in a small Cakchiquel Indian village and began translating the New Testament. His translation, with no modern tools, took only 11 years of work. Today it takes two well-trained linguists an average of 15 years to accomplish the same task. Townsend's accomplishment was likened by linguist Kenneth Pike to performing brain surgery with no formal training.

In addition to translating, Townsend supervised 20 Indian preachers and founded five schools, a clinic, a printing press, an orphanage, and a coffee cooperative. Through his over-diversification, Townsend adopted a principle for his organization of concentrating on the goal of Bible translation.

After being dragged before a town's mayor for distributing Bibles without permission, Townsend also grasped the principle of working in cooperation with national and local governments. Wycliffe linguists look upon themselves as guests and servants of the government where they work.

Now in heaven, Uncle Cam, as he is belovedly known, left a legacy that is committed to reaching 2,000 language groups by the year 2,000.

The 574 translation projects listed by the United Bible Societies in 1982 involved members of about 200 different denominations and missions. The World Home Bible League and the New York International Bible Society, for example, have now financed pioneer translations in 364 languages. Living Bibles International is currently producing popular-language translations in 110 countries. Special Bible translation organizations have begun within four different denominations in America.

Since Vatican II, the Roman Catholic Church has changed its attitude toward the use of vernacular languages, reading of Scripture by the laity, and the translation of the Bible. In 1982, Roman Catholics were actively involved in 133 translation projects.

The bulk of those translating are committed Christians, from all walks of life, who believe in the importance of giving the Scripture to people in their own language. Most have taken training in the Bible, in language learning and analysis, and in principles of translation.

Mother-tongue speakers of the language into which translation is being made are indispensable as "informants." In recent years a high percentage of translations are being done by national believers. Christians in Nigeria, Ghana, Brazil, the Philippines, Cameroon, Kenya, Korea, and Papua New Guinea have started national, Bible-translating organizations.

The Task Remaining

The ultimate goal of the Bible translation movement is for every person in the world to be able to read, or at least to hear, the Word of God in the language he understands best.

But how large is the remainder of the task? Of the 5,103 languages spoken in the world in 1978, 212 had a good Bible, 422 had a good New Testament, and 35 had Scripture which needed revision. In 830 languages, translation was in progress, but 168 languages were spoken by bilinguals who could use Scripture already available in another language and 154 were spoken only by people so old that they would probably be gone before a translation could be made.

That leaves 3,279 languages with nothing of God's Word yet available.

Computers speed up the language decoding and translation process. From a good translation in one language, a rough draft in another related language produced by computer can help a trained speaker of the second language produce a faithful yet readable translation sooner. Recently speakers of three different but related languages in Nigeria, working with an expatriate translation-consultant team, produced simultaneously New Testaments in the Izi, Eza, and Ikwo languages.

There is a growing number of experienced consultants, trained people who can explain the biblical text and evaluate the quality of a translation in another language, available to help the translators.

Translators now have at their disposal a wealth of books summarizing linguistic research and information theory, special exegetical helps, commentary compilations, a quarterly journal for translators, and computerized Greek lexicons and grammatical analyses. Computer and word processing equipment for manuscript preparation, typesetting, and proofreading are becoming routine.

History, Eric Fenn notes, shows that in countries like India, China, Burma, Korea, Japan, and Tibet, translation of the Scriptures "preceded the opening of the country to organized missionary work." The Scriptures have their own independent witness. People have come to faith through reading Scripture alone.

Churches have been started *without* missionaries, but *with* Scripture. The authors of *Church Growth in Latin America* tell of churches and congregations being established solely through the testimony of a Bible reader who had shared with others the reality of his discovery. "The pattern was clear: First a Bible, then a convert, then a church." But if the Bible is never translated, it will never be distributed.

Today mission strategists emphasize the need to plant churches in each people group and to work with the church until it has adequate members and resources to evangelize and exist without outside assistance. Other than the Holy Spirit, the only resource provided by God to make this possible is the Bible. Bible translation needs to be a consideration in every cross-cultural church planting program.

"There are a great many reasons why the world should have the Bible," William Nevins wrote over 100 years ago in *Practical Thoughts*. "I wonder that we who have the Bible and think so much of it, and have such means of multiplying and circulating copies of it, do not resolve at once to attempt, within a reasonable period, to give it to the world, since the world can only have it by the gift of those in whose possession it now is."

How many Bibles do you have at home in your language? How can we justify the more than 550 different English versions that have been made to date, when thousands of languages have *no* Scripture?

In spite of the availability of the Scriptures in over 1,700 languages, the Bible is still a closed book for speakers of almost twice that number of languages. For 3,279 language groups, the Bible has yet to become a book.

What part might God want you to play in the process?

12

Copies Solid Enough to Stand On

The Accuracy and Reliability of the Bible

If the Bible text has been garbled over the ages, how can we sort fact from fiction? If we only have flawed copies, it seems senseless to talk about a God-inspired, error-free Bible.

Are there really 200,000 errors in the old Bible manuscripts we have today?

Which of these troubling objections have you heard raised as you tried to share the Christian faith with someone? How would you answer them?

There *are* some good answers!

It can be solidly stated that the Bible comes into the modern world with more evidences of its accuracy and reliability than any other ancient document. That's a strong statement. What backs it up?

Comparison Texts
The Bible has the greatest number of ancient handwritten copies in its original languages available for comparison. There are approximately 750 manuscript copies of the Old

Testament in Hebrew and over 5,000 of the New Testament in Greek. In addition, there are over 9,000 ancient versions (translations from the original), 36,000 quotations by others in the ancient world (containing all but 11 verses of the New Testament), and about 2,000 church service books (called *lectionaries*, meaning "to read") which contain Scripture portions.

Other ancient documents rest on a far smaller copy base. Homer's *Iliad* has the most—643 copies. And the numbers run down from there. Sophocles has 100, Livy's *History of Rome* 20 (covering only 35 of the 142 original books), Caesar's *Gallic Wars* 10, and Tacitus' *Histories* 1 (containing only 4½ of the original 17 books). No one seriously challenges these secular works for having so few copies to compare.

Are there 200,000 errors in all those Bible manuscripts? Yes and no. It's more correct to talk about variations than errors, meaning differences among the copies. And the number of variations is actually quite small. To arrive at the large figure, each variation is counted all of the times it occurs. For example, if 1,267 manuscripts read "our Father" and the remainder have "your Father," this one letter change would count as 1,267 "errors" toward the total.

When the Masoretes recorded all known variations in the Hebrew Old Testament (three fourths of the Bible), they amounted to an average of one per page of text. Computer analysis of all the known New Testament manuscripts reveals only 0.1 percent variance. That means that 99.9 percent of the manuscripts' contents are in perfect agreement.

Most of the small percentage of actual differences are in spelling (such as the English "honour" versus "honor"), word order ("Paul the apostle" versus "the apostle Paul"), and grammar ("Father *who* art in heaven" versus "Father *which* art in heaven.) And *none* of the variations affects any basic doctrine.

Homer's *Iliad* is the next closest in textual purity, but it has a five percent textual corruption. That's fifty times greater percentage of its text varying—and that's based on far fewer copies than for the Bible. It would be reasonable to expect that as more copies of the *Iliad* are found, so would more variations.

The Bible also has copies closer to the time of writing. There exist complete copies of the Bible within 300 years of completion, most of it within 200 years, some books less than 100 years, and some fragments within a few decades.

To put those figures in perspective, the only extant copies of the writings of Thucydides and Herodotus are 1300 years later. The works of Tacitus and Caesar's *Gallic Wars* have a 900-year gap between time of writing and oldest known copy. All other ancient documents have larger gaps.

By any standard of comparison, the Bible copies are more reliable than any other known ancient documents!

No Misfires

The Bible prophets predicted the future. But so do modern ones like Jeanne Dixon.

Here are some tests for distinguishing true prophets. God, speaking to Moses, says:

> I will raise up for them a prophet like you from among their brothers; I will put my words in his mouth, and he will tell them everything I command him. If anyone does not listen to my words that the prophet speaks in my name, I myself will call him to account. But a prophet who presumes to speak in my name anything I have not commanded him to say, or a prophet who speaks in the name of other gods, must be put to death. You may say to yourselves, "How can we know when a message has not been spoken by the Lord?" If what a prophet proclaims in the name of the Lord does not take place or come true, that is a message the Lord has not spoken. That prophet has spoken presumptuously. Do not be afraid of him (Deut. 18:18-22).

A true prophet must be 100-percent accurate! By the best published rating, Jeanne has a 63-percent accuracy rate, impressive by human standards. But what if she were correct 80, 90, or even 99 percent of the time? How much error can be tolerated in an "authority" before it's considered unreliable? God tolerates none, and prescribed the death penalty for a false prophet in Moses' time!

God promised to give His prophets truth to tell and verification by miracles in addition to their every prediction coming true.

The Tyre Test

Of the hundreds of Bible prophecies which have come true and can be verified historically, consider one example pertaining to the ancient city of Tyre on the eastern Mediterranean coast west of Damascus (about halfway between Beirut and Haifa in Lebanon today.)

As we have seen, the Prophet Ezekiel wrote in Babylon in 597 B.C. or earlier. Underline at least seven specific prophecies found in his writing. The numbers are verse divisions for reference.

> ¹ In the eleventh year, on the first day of the month, the word of the Lord came to me: ² "Son of man, because Tyre has said of Jerusalem, 'Aha! The gate to the nations is broken, and its doors have swung open to me; now that she lies in ruins I will prosper,' ³ therefore this is what the Sovereign Lord says: I am against you, O Tyre, and I will bring many nations against you, like the sea casting up its waves. ⁴ They will destroy the walls of Tyre and pull down her towers; I will scrape away the rubble and make her a bare rock. ⁵ Out in the sea she will become a place to spread fishnets, for I have spoken, declares the Sovereign Lord. She will become plunder for the nations, ⁶ and her settlements on the mainland will be ravaged by the sword. Then they will know that I am the Lord. ⁷ For this is what the Sovereign Lord says: From the north I am going to bring against Tyre Nebuchadnezzar king of Babylon, king of kings, with horses and chariots, with

horsemen and a great army. [8] He will ravage your set-
tlements on the mainland with the sword; he will set
up siege works against you, build a ramp up to your
walls and raise his shield against you. . . .[9] He will direct
the blows of his battering rams against your walls and
demolish your towers with his weapons. [10] His horses
will be so many that they will cover you with dust.
Your walls will tremble at the noise of the war horses,
wagons and chariots when he enters your gates as men
enter a city whose walls have been broken through.
[11] The hoofs of his horses will trample all your streets;
he will kill your people with the sword, and your
strong pillars will fall to the ground. [12] They will plun-
der your wealth and loot your merchandise; they will
break down your walls and demolish your fine houses
and throw your stones, timber and rubble into the sea.
[13] I will put an end to your noisy songs, and the music
of your harps will be heard no more. [14] I will make you
a bare rock, and you will become a place to spread
fishnets. You will never be rebuilt, for I the Lord have
spoken, declares the Sovereign Lord. . . .[19] This is what
the Sovereign Lord says: When I make you a desolate
city, like cities no longer inhabited, and when I bring
the ocean depths over you and its vast waters cover
you, [20] then I will bring you down with those who go
down to the pit, to the people of long ago. I will make
you dwell in the earth below, as in ancient ruins, with
those who go down to the pit, and you will not return
or take your place in the land of the living. [21] I will
bring you to a horrible end and you will be no more.
You will be sought, but you will never again be found,
declares the Sovereign Lord" (Ezek. 26:1-14, 19-21).

Note among the specific, verifiable prophecies that:
- Many nations will be against Tyre (v. 3).
- Nebuchadnezzar will destroy mainland Tyre (v. 8).
- Tyre would be made a bare rock; flat like the top of rock
  (v. 4).

- Fishermen will spread nets over the site (v. 5).
- The city's debris will be thrown into water (v. 12).
- Tyre would never be rebuilt (v. 14).
- The destroyed city will never be found again (v. 21).

What Actually Happened?

The following account is condensed from historical records outside the Bible.

Twelve years after Ezekiel's prophecy, King Nebuchadnezzar of Babylon attacked the city of Tyre, whose great resistance led to 13 years of siege. When Nebuchadnezzar finally broke through the city gates, the city was nearly empty. During the 13-year siege, most of the townspeople moved by boat to a small island a half mile off the coast and built a fortified city there.

Nebuchadnezzar destroyed the original mainland city of Tyre in 573 B.C. But having no boats, the Babylonian army left. The new island city of Tyre remained a powerful city for almost 250 years thereafter. The Tyrians did not rebuild their old city on the coast.

In 333 B.C., Alexander the Great, bent on world conquest, was angered when he reached old Tyre and found no boats to reach the island city. Alexander ordered his soldiers to use the debris of old mainland Tyre to build a causeway 200 feet wide (60 meters) out to the island. Naturally, the people on the island put up great resistance, sabotaging by night what the Greeks built by day. Alexander had protective towers built and pushed ahead of his workers. But the men of Tyre burned them at night. When the rubble of the old city was exhausted, Alexander had his men dig up the building foundations and scrape the city's dust to extend his new causeway.

In 332, after seven months' work, Alexander's army reached the island, immediately killed 8,000 people of Tyre and sold 30,000 others into slavery.

Modern Tyre is where the island used to be, but now permanently joined to the mainland as a peninsula. Visitors to the coast where old Tyre used to be will see fishermen spreading out their nets to dry because it's such a smooth rocky place.

No Bible prophet ever misfired!

Calculating the Odds

The Old Testament contains 306 specific prophecies about Christ's first coming to earth, many of them mentioned earlier. Each one of them came true literally, exactly as predicted.

There are 540 Bible prophecies in both Testaments awaiting fulfillment at Jesus' second coming. What should we assume about them? (They will be literally fulfilled too!)

And the Bible contains hundreds of other prophecies about other things. Every one came true in the time and way it was scheduled.

What are the mathematical odds of the hundreds of Bible prophecies coming true? The answer is a number greater than the estimated stars in known space.

Professor Peter Stoner and others calculated the mathematical probabilities of just *eight* prophecies coming true and arrived at a conservative estimate of one chance out of a number with 26 zeroes (*Science Speaks,* Moody Press).

To visualize how big such a number is, imagine the state of Texas covered with silver dollars to a depth of three feet. Texas measures 710 miles by 760 miles and contains 262,134 square miles. Further imagine that one of those quintillions of silver dollars was temporarily painted red and a blindfolded person were asked to select one coin from anywhere within the state. What would be his "odds" of picking up the red one the first time? His chances of being correct the first time are the same as for eight Bible prophecies coming true!

Other Well-Picked Bones

Some modern scholars say Moses and the Israelites didn't go through the Red Sea, "correcting" the text to read the Reed Sea—a shallow swamp to the north.

If such a dubious change is correct, then God drowned the Egyptian Pharaoh's whole army in six inches of water!

Other unbelievers try to date the prophets' writings later to be after-the-fact histories instead of predictions. But in every case, they must fabricate another author and writing occasion. The original document then becomes a forgery—hardly reliable for history or prophecy!

The Prophet Jonah's reported ride inside a great fish or sea monster has been attacked as being scientifically impossible, that whales don't have gullets big enough to swallow a man whole and unharmed.

But the current *Encyclopedia Britannica* describes sperm whales with 20-foot gullets.

Supposedly a Christian, being pressed by an agnostic regarding Jonah, said, "When I get to heaven, I'll ask Jonah how it happened. But God said it happened, and I believe it."

Not believing there ever was a historical character named Jonah, the agnostic asked with an air of triumph, "And what if Jonah's not there?"

The tired and exasperated Christian answered, "Well Sir, then you ask him!"

The Bible has withstood every attack put upon it for nearly two millennia.

Many objections to the Bible's accuracy are arguments from silence. For nearly a century, critics condemned the Bible's 40 mentions of the Hittites, a people then unknown to secular history. But missionary William Wright found the first Hittite inscriptions and relics in 1872. By 1900 so much had been uncovered that scholars admitted that this ancient empire was once as powerful as the Egyptians' and Assyrians'. Today the University of Chicago offers a major in Hittitology!

The archeologists' spades have overturned dozens of similar objections.

The eighteenth-century French skeptic Voltaire boasted, "One hundred years from my day there will not be a Bible in the earth except one that is looked upon by an antiquarian curiosity-seeker," while his works would be found in every household. But 50 years after Voltaire's death, the Geneva Bible Society purchased the infidel's old home and moved in presses to print the Word of God! Two hundred years later, on Christmas Eve 1933, the British government paid the Russian government $510,000 for one copy of the Bible in Greek—Codex Sinaiticus. That same day a first edition of Voltaire sold in Paris for 11 cents.

Frank Morison, an English lawyer, set out to disprove the Bible. He felt if he could discredit the resurrection of Christ, the Bible and Christianity could be summarily dismissed. As he studied the historical evidence, putting his best intellect to the case, he became overwhelmed by the facts and was converted to faith in Christ. Morison's story is recorded in his book *Who Moved the Stone?* (InterVarsity Press).

The Real Issue

For many, such issues are not intellectual questions so much as moral ones. Every skeptic I've gotten to know has had close contact with evangelical Christianity in the past, then turned away from it. For they rightly realize that if the Bible is indeed God's Word, as it claims, such an authority requires obedience. Many consciences are soothed temporarily by attacking the truth source.

I believe the Bible is literally true. In the original manuscripts God never stuttered once. And the copies of those sacred documents have been supernaturally preserved. To hold a faithful translation in English, such as the KJV, is to hold the very Words of God.

Don't ask me how to explain how the holy God could use sinful men to write a perfect Book. Nor could I explain how the holy God could use a sinful woman (Mary acknowledged her need of a Saviour, as we all must) to produce the perfect body of the Son of God, the Lord Jesus Christ.

Trying to explain such things is like trying to unscrew the inscrutable!

It's all a question of authority. The Bible will stand through all eternity as the absolute truth of God whether puny people recognize it or not.

But everyone is called upon to make a decision. Humans

are not robots; God doesn't force them to submit to His authority. But the losers are those who choose not to live under His authority. They are cast upon a limitless sea of uncertainty and become entangled in a downward moral spiral. In the last of his 13 New Testament letters, the Apostle Paul describes the life of those who reject the authority of God and His Word in their lives.

But mark this: There will be terrible times in the last days. People will be lovers of themselves, lovers of money, boastful, proud, abusive, disobedient to their parents, ungrateful, unholy, without love, unforgiving, slanderous, without self-control, brutal, not lovers of the good, treacherous, rash, conceited, lovers of pleasure rather than lovers of God—having a form of godliness but denying its power. Have nothing to do with them. They are the kind who worm their way into homes and gain control over weak-willed women, who are loaded down with sins and are swayed by all kinds of evil desires, always learning but never able to come to acknowledge the truth. Just as Jannes and Jambres opposed Moses, so also these men oppose the truth—men of depraved minds, who, as far as the faith is concerned, are rejected. But they will not get very far because, as in the case of those men, their folly will be clear to everyone (2 Tim. 3:1-10).

Do these 2,000-year-old words sound modern?

What Benefits Are Offered?
Catch the contrast as God continues to speak through Paul.

But as for you, continue in what you have learned and have become convinced of, because you know those from whom you learned it, and how from infancy you have known the holy Scriptures, which are able to make you wise for salvation through faith in Christ Jesus. All Scripture is God-breathed and is useful for teaching, rebuking, correcting and training in righteousness, so that the man of God may be thoroughly equipped for every good work. In the presence of God and of Christ Jesus, who will judge the living and the dead, and in view of his appearing and his kingdom, I give you this charge: Preach the word, be prepared in season and out of season; correct, rebuke and encourage—with great patience and careful instruction. For the time will come when men will not put up with sound doctrine. Instead, to suit their own desires, they will gather around them a great number of teachers to say what their itching ears want to hear. They will turn their ears away from the truth and turn aside to myths (2 Tim. 3:14–4:4).

Paul says the Scriptures contain convincing truths we can be certain about, words which produce wisdom in us, and lead us to salvation through faith in Christ Jesus. The Bible words were breathed out by God Himself, designed to make us complete, mature, and adequate for life and every good work He has planned for us.

Reading and studying the Bible satisfies one of God's basic requirements for us. When God gives us commands, He always has our best interests in mind. This passage gives us four benefits the Bible can bring us. The first is positive: to teach us the faith. The Bible gives us truth to believe. Only the Bible gives authoritative answers to life's basic questions: Who am I? Where did I come from? Where am I going? What is the purpose of life?

The second Bible benefit is negative: to serve as a rebuke—to correct false philosophies and pagan ideas picked up en route through life. It is because the Bible tells us what is wrong with us that so many try to discount the Bible.

The third Bible study benefit is also negative: correction. This involves resetting the direction of our lives. God's Word not only shows us where we are going astray, but it also shows us how to get right with God and gives us steps to correct our life course. The process may be painful, like resetting a broken bone. But the ultimate goal is worth it.

The fourth benefit is positive: to help us do what is right. The Bible can train us in righteousness or good living. The ultimate result is that we may be men and women of God who are fully equipped for every good work God has for us. We don't have to be limited to doing what comes naturally. Through the power of God and His Word in us, we can do what comes supernaturally!

Other books are written by people for our information; the Bible was written by God for our transformation!

If we really believe the Bible is final truth, God's authority, then how significant a place does it have in our lives? How often do we read it? How much do we think about it? How diligent are we at committing parts of it to memory?

If today each of us were asked to think of one thing we could do that would please God the most, we probably wouldn't be at a loss for an answer.

You see, most of us don't need more revelation from God; we only need to decide to *do* what we already know to be right.

It's not a matter of the mind so much as the will.

APPENDIX A

Abbreviations

ASV *American Standard Version of the Bible*
Col. *Book of Colossians*
Dan. *Book of Daniel*
Deut. *Book of Deuteronomy*
Ecc. *Book of Ecclesiastes*
Eph. *Book of Ephesians*
ERV *English Revised Version of the Bible*
Es. *Book of Esther*
Ex. *Book of Exodus*
Ezek. *Book of Ezekiel*
1 Chron. *Book of 1 Chronicles*
1 Cor. *Book of 1 Corinthians*
1 Sam. *Book of 1 Samuel*
1 Thes. *Book of 1 Thessalonians*
1 Tim. *Book of 1 Timothy*
Gal. *Book of Galatians*
Gen. *Book of Genesis*
GNB *Good News Bible*
Hab. *Book of Habakkuk*
Hag. *Book of Haggai*
Heb. *Book of Hebrews*
Isa. *Book of Isaiah*
Jer. *Book of Jeremiah*
Josh. *Book of Joshua*
Jud. *Book of Judges*
KJV *King James Version of the Bible*
Lam. *Book of Lamentations*
Lev. *Book of Leviticus*
LXX *Septuagint (Greek Old Testament)*
Mal. *Book of Malachi*
Matt. *Book of Matthew*

NASB *New American Standard Bible*
Neh. *Book of Nehemiah*
NIV *Holy Bible, New International Version*
NKJV *The New King James Version of the Bible*
Num. *Book of Numbers*
Obad. *Book of Obadiah*
Phil. *Book of Philippians*
Phile. *Book of Philemon*
Prov. *Book of Proverbs*
Ps. *Book of Psalms, Psalm*
Pss. *Psalms*
Rev. *Book of Revelation*
Rom. *Book of Romans*
RSV *Revised Standard Version of the Bible*
2 Chron. *Book of Chronicles*
2 Cor. *Book of 2 Corinthians*
2 Sam. *Book of 2 Samuel*
2 Thes. *Book of 2 Thessalonians*
2 Tim. *Book of 2 Timothy*
TLB *The Living Bible*
TR *Textus Receptus ("Received" Greek New Testament)*
WBT *Wycliffe Bible Translators*
Zech. *Book of Zechariah*
Zeph. *Book of Zephaniah*

APPENDIX B

Recommended Resources

General

Alexander, Pat. *The Lion Encyclopedia of the Bible.* Batavia, Ill.: Lion USA, 1986.

Beale, David. *A Pictorial History of Our English Bible.* Greenville, S.C.: Bob Jones University Press, 1982.

Bruce, F.F. *The Books and the Parchments.* Old Tappan, N.J.: Revell, 1963.

Ewert, David. *From Ancient Tablets to Modern Translations: A General Introduction to the Bible.* Grand Rapids: Zondervan, 1986.

Geisler, Norman L., and William E. Nix. *From God to Us: How We Got Our Bible.* Chicago: Moody Press, 1974.

Lightfoot, Neil. *How We Got the Bible.* Grand Rapids: Baker Book House, 1988.

Chapter 1—The Bible's Uniqueness among the World's Books

Campbell, R.K. *Our Wonderful Bible.* Snydertown, Pa.: Believers Bookshelf, n.d.

Criswell, W.A. *Why I Preach That the Bible Is Literally True.* Grand Rapids: Zondervan, 1969.

Packer, J.I. *Beyond the Battle for the Bible.* Westchester, Ill.: Crossway Books, 1980.

Chapters 2–5—The Old Testament Writers

Archer, Gleason. *A Survey of Old Testament Introduction.* Chicago: Moody Press, 1973.

Wilkinson, Bruce, and Kenneth Boa. *Talk Through the Old Testament.* Nashville: Nelson, 1983.

Chapters 6, 9—Collecting the Old and New Testament Books

McDowell, Josh. *Evidence That Demands a Verdict, Vol. II.* San Bernardino: Campus Crusade, 1981.

Metzger, Bruce M. *An Introduction to the Apocrypha.* New York: Oxford University Press, 1957.

Metzger, Bruce M. *The Text of the New Testament.* New York: Oxford University Press, 1964.

Chapters 7–8—The New Testament Writers

Metzger, Bruce M. *The New Testament: Its Background, Growth, and Content.* Nashville: Abingdon, 1965.

Wilkinson, Bruce, and Kenneth Boa. *Talk Through the New Testament.* Nashville: Nelson, 1983.

Chapter 10—Putting the Bible into English

Bruce, F.F. *A History of the Bible in English.* New York: Oxford University Press, 1978.

Fuller, David Otis. *Which Bible?* Grand Rapids: Kregel, 1984.

Kohlenberger, John III. *Words about the Word: A Guide to Choosing and Using Your Bible*. Grand Rapids: Zondervan, 1987.

Kubo, Sakae, and Walter Specht. *So Many Versions?* Grand Rapids: Zondervan, 1983.

Chapter 11—Getting the Bible into Other Languages

Hefley, James and Marti. *Uncle Cam*. Milford, Mich.: Mott Media, 1981.

Moore, Hyatt, ed. *Pass the Word: Fifty Years of Wycliffe Bible Translators*. Huntington Beach, Calif.: Wycliffe, 1984.

Wallis, Ethel E., and Mary Bennett. *Two Thousand Tongues to Go*. New York: Harper and Row, 1959.

Chapter 12—The Accuracy and Reliability of the Bible

Bruce, F.F. *The New Testament Documents: Are They Reliable?* Grand Rapids: Eerdmans, 1959.

Little, Paul. *Know Why You Believe*. Wheaton: Victor Books, 1984.

MacArthur, John, Jr. *Why I Trust the Bible*. Wheaton: Victor Books, 1983.

McDowell, Josh. *Evidence That Demands a Verdict*. San Bernardino: Campus Crusade for Christ, 1979.

Womack, Tom, ed. *Celebrating the Word*. Portland, Ore.: Multnomah Press, 1987.

Atlases

Beitzel, Barry J. *The Moody Atlas of Bible Lands.* Chicago, Moody Press, 1985.

Rand McNally Family World Atlas. Chicago: Rand McNally, 1988.

INDEX